SPECIAL OFFER
MADE ONLY TO BUYERS OF THE
FAMOUS BRANDS
COOKBOOK LIBRARY

BEAUTIFUL CORNING PRODUCTS

A Corning Ware® French White® 1½-Quart Oval Casserole with Glass Cover—retail value $23.00—yours FREE with 12 Proofs of Purchase (one from each volume) and $4.00 to cover postage and handling

and

By special arrangement, the COOKBOOK LIBRARY also offers incredible dollars off other selected Corning products, with total savings of up to $143.05.

Choose any—or all—of three Corning sets:

**Visions® Rangetop
1½-Quart Covered Saucepan and
2½-Quart Covered Saucepan**
Coupons available in Volumes 1 through 4
Retail Value $42.00
With 1 Coupon $29.95
With 2 Coupons $25.95
With 3 Coupons $21.95
postage and handling included

**Thermique® 1-Liter Thermal Server with
4 Ceramic Mugs**
Coupons available in Volumes 5 through 8
Retail Value $46.00
With 1 Coupon $31.95
With 2 Coupons $27.95
With 3 Coupons $23.95
postage and handling included

**Corning Ware® French White® 14-Piece
Cookware**
Coupons available in Volumes 9 through 1
Retail Value $155.90
With 1 Coupon $ 74.95
With 2 Coupons $ 64.95
With 3 Coupons $ 54.95
postage and handling included

PROOF OF PURCHASE COUPON
for free Corning Ware®
French White® Covered Casserole
RETAIL VALUE $23.00

F 1-4

PROOF OF PURCHASE COUPON
Visions® Rangetop 4-piece Cookware
RETAIL VALUE $42.00

V 1-4   **VOL. #1, VOL. #2, VOL. #3, VOL. #4,**

FRENCH WHITE® COOKWARE
1½-Qt. Oval Casserole with Glass Cover

RETAIL VALUE: **$23.00**

THERMIQUE® THERMAL SERVER AND MUG SET

RETAIL VALUE: **$46.00**

VISIONS® RANGETOP COOKWARE
4-Piece Saucepan Set

RETAIL VALUE: **$42.00**

FRENCH WHITE® COOKWARE SET

2½-Quart Covered Round Casserole,
10" Pie Plate (Quiche),
2½-Quart Covered Oval Casserole, 1½-Quart
Covered Round Casserole,
1½-Quart Open Oval Casserole, 1-Quart Oval
Vegetable Dish,
8½" Pie Plate (Quiche), Two 15-Ounce
Individual Oval Casseroles,
and Two 16-Ounce Individual Round Casseroles

RETAIL VALUE: **$155.90**

To Order Other Volumes

If you would like to order extra volumes of the FAMOUS BRANDS COOKBOOK LIBRARY (if for any reason you have been unable to purchase any volume of the FAMOUS BRANDS COOKBOOK LIBRARY, or if you want additional copies for yourself or for giving as gifts), you may do so by sending a check or money order for the retail price plus $2.00 for postage and handling to:

Brand Name Publishing Corporation
1950 Craig Road
St. Louis, Missouri 63146
(Missouri residents add applicable sales tax)

Volume 1	**Desserts**	$1.99 plus $2.00 postage
Volume 2	**Every Oven Microwave Cookbook**	$3.99 plus $2.00 postage
Volume 3	**Great Vegetable Dishes**	$3.99 plus $2.00 postage
Volume 4	**Meat Cookbook**	$3.99 plus $2.00 postage
Volume 5	**Chicken & Poultry**	$3.99 plus $2.00 postage
Volume 6	**Breads, Quick Breads & Coffee Cakes**	$3.99 plus $2.00 postage
Volume 7	**Soups & Salads**	$3.99 plus $2.00 postage
Volume 8	**Pasta Dishes**	$3.99 plus $2.00 postage
Volume 9	**Fish & Seafood**	$3.99 plus $2.00 postage
Volume 10	**Cooking with Eggs & Cheese**	$3.99 plus $2.00 postage
Volume 11	**Main Dishes**	$3.99 plus $2.00 postage
Volume 12	**Chocolate Classics**	$3.99 plus $2.00 postage

Contents

A Fresh Look at Vegetables

Unfortunately—not for them, but for us—vegetables are the poor relations of the food world. They are often ignored, or considered only as an afterthought, more often eaten as a duty than as a pleasure. No spouse comes home, peeks into the pots on the stove, and cries, "Oh, good—spinach! My favorite!" No child is likely to plead, "Mommy, fix carrots for supper, please." Most home cooks, planning a very special dinner, don't start with cauliflower and build the menu around it.

And that's too bad. Vegetables are good for us, and they're also very good eating. But endlessly served boiled, with a dab of butter, they can become pretty tiresome. The thought of such a dish causes no excitement, as a big, juicy steak will, or a three-layer devil's food cake with sea foam frosting. Even fruit has it all over vegetables when it comes to stirring up the appetite. A big, perfect, blush-cheeked peach can make the poets sing. But who ever paints word pictures of one perfect parsnip?

What to do? Start a pro-veg campaign and set our imaginations to work. Give vegetables the importance they deserve. How? Bypass the awful sameness, learn to cook vegetables in new ways, work out different combinations, seek out sauces and seasonings that will make the meal's vegetables something to look forward to.

There are dozens of things to do to and with vegetables that will successfully elevate their looks and flavor. Begin by looking around at the greengrocery or the produce section of your supermarket for vegetables you've never served before. Try new greens: mustard, beet, kale. New tubers: parsnips, jícama, jerusalem artichokes. Experiment with cooking celery instead of serving it raw, serving cauliflower raw instead of cooked. There are treats in store for you and your family if you've never tried Brussels sprouts or finocchio or leeks.

Vegetable cookery is a challenge. With the help of this book you can meet it and win your family over to the subtle delights of well-cooked, well-served vegetables and fresh, crisp raw ones. All it takes is know-how, and that know-how is waiting for you right here.

Supermarket Shopper

Artichokes: Fresh artichokes are available the year around, but the peak season is the months of March, April, and May. There is virtually no relationship between size and quality, so choose a size suitable for your purpose. Select solid, heavy-for-their-size artichokes without any loose or spread or discolored leaves—signs that old age is setting in. They should be a pleasant deep green. Pass by any that are pale or that have extensive purplish-brown blemishes.

One large globe artichoke makes one serving—remember that one of an artichoke's least lovable features is the amount of garbage it engenders. If you are going to use only the hearts—the cluster of small pale leaves in the center, plus the smooth, mealy artichoke bottom—count on 4 to 6 hearts to make a serving. If you are going to use only the bottoms, you'll want to choose very large artichokes. Two bottoms—they are generally offered filled with some savory preparation—will serve one person, or one such filled bottom if it is used as an edible garnish rather than an integral part of the meal.

Asparagus: Look for fresh-appearing, crisp stalks and tightly closed heads. Wrinkled or twisted stalks and/or open heads indicate overmaturity and mean that the vegetable will be tough, stringy, and lacking in the fresh flavor that is so delicious. Avoid asparagus that is excessively sandy. The sand works its way insidiously into the heads and scales, is exceedingly difficult to wash out, and is the bane of the dedicated asparagus eater.

Asparagus is sold loose, by the pound, or in bunches that generally weigh in the neighborhood of a little over 2 pounds. Two pounds will serve 4 to 6. Bunches are held together prosaically with rubber bands or sometimes with red tape. Medium-size asparagus averages between 16 and 20 stalks per pound. As is true of all fresh foods, apsaragus is most expensive at the beginning and end of the 5-month season (February-June), least expensive at the season's peak (April-May).

Beans: Inspect green or wax beans for fresh-looking pods, pleasingly plump but not too fat—great bulk means the beans are overmature. These snap beans are available all year, but are at their peak from late spring to early fall. Pods should snap easily, be straight and nicely colored, without scars or rusty-looking spots. Select reasonably uniform beans so they'll all be done at the same time. One pound of green or wax beans will yield about 3 cups cooked.

Lima beans, both the big ones and the babies, are also available all year, with the largest supplies in the market from June to September. The shelled ones should be shiny, a uniformly pale, springy green, and look as if they were bursting their skins with pride. When you buy soy or lima or fava beans to shell yourself, look for clean, unblemished pods—and feel them to make sure there are beans within, for you can sometimes get a nasty surprise. Beans of any kind that feel damp or slimy are well on their way to decay. Two pounds of lima or fava beans in the pod will yield about 2¼ cups shelled and cooked.

Beets: Choose firm, shapely, unblemished beets that show good color. The smaller they are, the more tender they will be. Count on about 1½ pounds to make 4 servings.

Broccoli: Select fresh-looking, unblemished bunches with compact heads, which may be dark green, dark gray-green, or purplish-green. Stalks and branches should be firm but not hard, and should not feel spongy or woody. If the heads are yellow or opened, the vegetable is old. Look at the ends of the stalks. If they are turning brown or look slimy, the broccoli has been in the market too long.

Brussels Sprouts: Brussels sprouts are sold loose by the pound, or in small baskets like those in which strawberries come. A pound will make 4 servings. Look for small, compact, firm heads that are uniformly green. Brussels sprouts with yellow leaves are old; they will have poor flavor. If you pick out your own, choose heads of uniform size—the smaller the better—so all will cook at the same rate.

Cabbage: Look for firm heads, solid and heavy for their size (particularly Danish and domestic). Pass by any with yellowed or browned leaves. Cabbages with split heads have been left too long before picking—skip them, too.

Carrots: Purchase carrots loose, by the pound—a pound will yield 2½ cups when cooked, make 3 to 4 servings—or in plastic bags. Either way, look for shapely firmness, a fresh, clean look, and a good golden-orange color. Pass by any with blemishes or soft spots. Carrots that have split or those that have forked into two ends may be woody, so may carrots with a dry, too-pale, flaky appearance. Carrots begin to rot at both the root and the stem ends—make certain that those you buy are solid and not starting to turn brown in those places. If the tops are still on the carrots, they should be fresh and green.

Cauliflower: Choose a head that is heavy for its size, firm and compact. The size of the head bears no relation to its quality or age. The condition of the leaves—green and fresh-looking, or yellow, withering, and limp—is a guide. Avoid bruises and more than a minimum of brown spots, as well as a head that is darkening and seems to be shrinking in upon itself. This condition is called "riciness" and is a sign of old age.

Celery: Celery should be so crisp it snaps at you. Choose such stalks, making certain the leaves are fresh-looking and have not begun to wilt. When you get the celery home, don't make the mistake of whacking off the tops and throwing them away—in them lies a bouquet of delicious flavor for soups and other cooked foods, and a bonus of pretty leaves for garnishing.

Corn: If you're a resident of the suburbs, not too far from a farmer who grows his own sweet corn, you're in luck. Learn his schedule of picking times and be waiting—it's not polite to shove—to rush the corn home, strip it, and cook it. That way, you'll discover how wonderful corn at its best can be.

Lacking such a blissful circumstance, you can still enjoy the gustatory delight of fresh sweet corn if you shop wisely for it. The season lasts from May—in most places, there is corn shipped in from Florida—to the beginning of September, when the last local corn is picked in the East and Midwest; again, there may be shipped-in corn available until December. For the best choice, get to the supermarket in the morning. Choose ears with fresh-looking, clean green husks and golden-brown silk that is not wet and matted but has a look of life to it. Pull back the husk and look at the kernels—they should be plump and evenly full, never dry looking. Kernels can be white or yellow, but the old-fashioned white types such as country gentleman and shoepeg, once most popular, are no longer considered as desirable as the yellow kinds, the new and improved relatives of golden bantam.

Eggplant: Choose eggplants heavy for their size, with smooth unblemished skin. Rough, spongy places are a sign of poor quality, brown spots indicate incipient decay.

Mushrooms: Normal color is white to a pallid brown, depending on the area in which you live. Look for caps that are closed (not spread wide, with cracks marring the circumference), that are clean, that feel firm to light pressure. The gills—the flutings between cap and stem—should be free from the stem, and look crowded; in small mushrooms they are white, but range from pinkish to brown-black as size increases. The stem should be thick, solid, and smooth except for the fuzzy ring that marks the place where the mushroom pushed up out of the earth or other medium in which it was grown. Count on 1 pound of fresh mushrooms to furnish 4 cups sliced, raw; a pound will yield 20 to 24 medium-size caps, with a bonus of stems for soups and sauces.

Small mushrooms are least expensive—choose them for chopping and slicing. Those with long stems are usually cheaper than the shorter ones, because caps are more tender than stems. Medium-size mushrooms can be sliced for salads, for sautéing, to stuff for appetizer servings. The very big ones—3 inches or more in diameter—are just right to stuff as a main or side dish.

Okra: Look for fresh-colored pods that spring back to the touch, that have an air of youth and crispness; they should be no more than 4 inches in length. Snap one—it should snap easily, and its seeds should be fairly firm but yielding, in no way hard. Avoid shriv-eled, limp pods, dull color, soft spots.

Onions: Dry onions are most often sold by the pound; the big ones, such as Bermudas, may be sold by the pound or the piece, shallots by the bag or the box, green onions and leeks by the bunch, chives by the bunch or pot. Also available, particularly around the holiday season, may be very small white onions, often labeled "boiling onions," by the bag or box, to be served as a vegetable side dish.

Choose dry onions, of whatever size or color, that are bright looking and absolutely solid, without any softness; softness and/or dark color, particularly at the root end, indicate oncoming spoilage. Fresh onions—green, leeks, chives—should be clean and green of foliage, with no wet/slippery texture, no turning-yellow color.

Peas: Choose velvety, nearly unblemished pods, well-filled but not looking as if they were about to burst. The peas should not rattle in their pods—if they do, they're old and tough. Color should be bright green and, of course, avoid damp or slimy peas, and those with damaged pods. One pound of fresh peas will yield 1 cup after shelling.

Peppers: The pepper should look fresh, be of the proper color for its kind, and have no soft or pale spots, which tell you that decay is setting in. Limp or shriveled peppers should be avoided, as should badly misshapen ones. They are available all year around, but the peak season is June through September.

Potatoes: To calculate servings: 3 medium baking potatoes equals 1 pound; 1 pound potatoes equals 4 servings mashed, 4 to 5 servings French fried, 2 cups cubes or slices. Choose potatoes that are reasonably clean, that are firm and smooth, with regular shape so there won't be too much lost in peeling. Avoid those with wilted, wrinkled skin, soft dark areas, cuts in the skin, and those that have begun to sprout. Never buy potatoes with a green tinge—they may be bitter, and some people are allergic to the chemical that produces the green color.

Spinach: Fresh spinach can be bought in bulk, by the pound, or—washed and trimmed—in plastic bags. In either case, the leaves should not be yellowed but have a freshly dark green look, and may be flat-leaf or crinkled variety. Wilt, decay, crushed leaves, and signs of insect damage should indicate to you spinach not worth your trouble.

Squash: Make certain that the squash is solid, without soft spots, that it is of proper size and color for its kind. Avoid squash with cuts or other breaks in the skin. Summer varieties should be young, have tender skins. Both summer and winter squash should be heavy for their size.

Sweet Potatoes: Choose potatoes of good shape—and uniform size if you are going to bake them—without blemishes, pleasingly plump, clean and dry.

Beautiful Bits
and Bites

Buffet foods, hors d'oeuvres, snacks—vegetables make great less-than-a-full meal treats, by themselves or served with flavorful sauces and dips.

Zippy Vegetable Dip

Makes about 1½ cups

  1 package (8 ounces) cream cheese, softened
  ¼ cup finely chopped celery
  ¼ cup chopped seeded cucumber
  1 tablespoon finely chopped onion
 10 drops hot pepper sauce
  ¼ cup Wish-Bone® Deluxe French or Sweet 'n Spicy French Dressing

In medium bowl, combine all ingredients; blend well. Chill.

Spicy Dip for Vegetables

Makes 1¼ cups

  ¼ cup Sun-Maid® Seedless Raisins
  1 cup cream-style cottage cheese
  2 tablespoons cider vinegar
  ½ small onion, cut up
  1 teaspoon chili powder
  ½ to ¾ teaspoon curry powder
  ¾ teaspoon salt
  ⅛ teaspoon freshly ground black pepper
    Crisp fresh vegetables for dipping

Place raisins in a small bowl and cover with hot tap water. Let stand 10 minutes. Meanwhile, in blender container, combine cottage cheese, vinegar, onion, chili powder, curry, salt, and pepper. Add drained, soaked raisins. Cover and blend at high speed until smooth and creamy. If necessary, add 1 tablespoon water in which raisins were soaked (or water) to make a good dipping consistency. Serve well chilled with a selection of vegetables, such as cauliflowerets, carrot sticks, blanched green beans, radish roses, broccoli, celery sticks, zucchini sticks, or cooked artichokes.

Black Bean Dip

Makes 2½ cups

  1 can (10½ ounces) condensed black bean soup, undiluted
  1 can (8 ounces) tomato sauce
  ½ to 1 cup shredded sharp cheddar cheese
  ¼ teaspoon chili powder
    Crackers or corn chips

Combine soup, tomato sauce, ½ cup of the cheese and chili powder in saucepan. Cook at medium heat until the cheese has melted. Add more shredded cheese until the mixture is as thick as desired. Serve from electric skillet or saucepan kept warm on an electric trivet or candle. Serve with crackers or corn chips.

Vegetable Hors d'Oeuvres

Vegetable hors d'oeuvres can be more innovative than celery and carrot sticks. The newest way to serve vegetables is as a base for a variety of fillings. Substituting vegetables for the usual bread or cracker base will give you hors d'oeuvres with more visual appeal and texture contrast. For example, cut cherry tomatoes into 4 wedges, cutting not quite all the way through. Open out and stuff with a small cube of jellied cranberry sauce; sprinkle with chopped chives. Tiny tomatoes can also be filled with a dollop of pesto sauce or a rolled anchovy. Snow peas can be topped with a piping of low-calorie cream cheese mixed with chives and dusted with curry powder. Or, top cucumber cups with shrimp and red caviar. Endive spears, filled with ratatouille or deviled ham makes a delicious change. Finally, cut large carrots lengthwise into thin slices using a vegetable peeler, then spread with a thin layer of cranorange relish or whole-berry cranberry sauce.

These are only a few suggestions, but the possibilities here are almost limitless.

South of the Border Dip

Makes 1 cup
    1 medium avocado, peeled and cubed
    2 tomatoes, peeled, seeded and cubed
    3 green pepper rings, ½ inch wide
    ½ medium onion, sliced
    2 tablespoons lime juice
    ½ teaspoon dry mustard
    ½ teaspoon Worcestershire sauce
       Dash Tabasco pepper sauce
    ½ teaspoon salt
       Corn chips

Combine all ingredients in blender. Cover and process at Cream 1 minute. Serve with corn chips.

California Cocktail Dip

Makes about 1½ cups
    ¾ cup Wish-Bone® Creamy Cucumber Dressing
    ¾ cup sour cream
    1 tablespoon chopped parsley
    ¼ teaspoon dry mustard

In small bowl, combine all ingredients; blend well. Chill.

Green Onion Canapés

Makes 1¾ cups
    1 package (8 ounces) cream cheese, softened
    ½ cup chopped green onions
    ¼ cup Hellmann's or Best Foods Real Mayonnasie
       Assorted crackers
       Ripe olive slices or red caviar

In small bowl with mixer at high speed, beat cream cheese until light and fluffy. Beat in onions and mayonnaise until well mixed. Cover; chill at least 4 hours to blend flavors. Pipe or spread on crackers. Garnish with ripe olive slices or red caviar.

Hummus

Makes 2 cups
    ¼ cup tahini (sesame paste)
    ¼ cup lemon juice
    3 tablespoons olive oil
    1 or 2 cloves garlic, halved
    1 can (20 ounces) chick-peas or garbanzo beans,
       drained
    ½ teaspoon salt
       Dash pepper
       Dash Cayenne pepper
       Chopped parsley

Put tahini, lemon juice, oil, and garlic into blender container. Cover; blend at high speed until smooth. While blender is running, tip center cap and gradually add chick-peas, blending until smooth. If necessary, stop blender during processing and push ingredients toward blades with rubber spatula. Add salt, pepper, and Cayenne and blend well until mixed. Turn into serving dish; sprinkle with chopped parsley. Chill.

Lipton California Dip

Makes about 2 cups
    1 envelope Lipton® Onion Recipe Soup Mix
    2 cups sour cream

In small bowl, blend Lipton Onion Recipe Soup Mix with sour cream; chill.

California Vegetable Dip
Add 1 cup each finely chopped green pepper and tomato and 2 teaspoons chili powder.

California Blue Cheese Dip
Add ¼ pound crumbled blue cheese and ¼ cup finely chopped walnuts.

California Seafood Dip
Add 1 cup finely chopped cooked shrimp, clams, or crabmeat, ¼ cup chili sauce; and 1 tablespoon horseradish.

California Horseradish 'n' Bacon Dip
Add 6 slices bacon, crisp-cooked and crumbled, and 3 tablespoons horseradish.

Skinny California Dip
Substitute 2 cups (16 ounces) plain yogurt for sour cream.

Chili Bean Dip

Makes about 1⅔ cups

  1 can (1 pound) Heinz Vegetarian Beans in
    Tomato Sauce, drained
  1 package (3 ounces) cream cheese, softened
1½ teaspoons chili powder
  1 tablespoon minced green onion, including stem
    Corn chips or raw vegetables

Combine beans, cream cheese, and chili powder in blender. Purée until smooth and creamy. Stir in onion. Cover; chill to blend flavors. Serve with corn chips or raw chilled vegetables.

Spinach Dip

Makes 2½ cups

  1 package (10 ounces) frozen chopped spinach,
    thawed
½ cup snipped parsley
  1 bottle (8 ounces) Seven Seas® Green Goddess
    Dressing
  1 cup (8 ounces) sour cream
    Raw vegetables, cut in bite-size pieces

Remove all liquid from spinach. Stir in parsley and dressing. Fold in sour cream. Chill. Serve with vegetables.

Last-Minute Bean Dip

Makes 3½ cups

  1 can (28 ounces) pork and beans
¾ cup (3 ounces) shredded cheddar cheese
  3 tablespoons Durkee RedHot! Sauce
1½ teaspoons Durkee Chili Powder
1½ teaspoons Durkee Garlic Salt
  6 slices bacon, fried crisp and crumbled
    Tortilla or corn chips (optional)

Blend pork and beans in blender or food processor (½ can at a time) until partially puréed; place in saucepan. Add remaining ingredients except bacon; heat through. Sprinkle with bacon before serving. Serve with tortilla or corn chips.

It's Spreadable and Stuffable!

Makes about 2 cups

½ cup sour cream
  1 package (8 ounces) cream cheese, softened
  1 envelope Lipton® Onion-Mushroom Recipe
    Soup Mix
    Variations (recipes follow)

In medium bowl, thoroughly blend sour cream with cream cheese; stir in Lipton Onion-Mushroom Recipe Soup Mix and *one* variation; chill.

Note: Try as a spread for crackers, party-size bread or bread cutouts; or, try as a stuffing for raw mushroom caps, celery sticks, green pepper wedges or cherry tomatoes.

Variations

Mexicali Olé

Add ½ cup each chopped green pepper and celery, ¼ cup chopped drained pimiento, and 1½ teaspoons chili powder.

Pick-a-Dilly Shrimp

Add 1 can (4½ ounces) small shrimp, drained and chopped, and 1 teaspoon dill weed.

India Curry

Add 4 chopped hard-cooked eggs and 1 teaspoon curry powder.

Don't Forget to Eat the Garnish

A lonely sprig of parsley often comes from the restaurant kitchen, placed on a plate as a garnish to brighten the food being served; all too often, it goes back to the kitchen as well, the rest of the food eaten but the parsley ignored. This is a habit that should be changed. Parsley is low in calories, rich in vitamins A and C, and in potassium and iron; besides, it has a delicious flavor. So good, indeed, that it deserves to be upgraded from the garnish to the eat-it-all vegetable class. To keep parsley for a number of days at home, wash it well, shake it dry, then place it in a glass of water as if it were a bouquet. Put it, glass and all, in a plastic bag and secure airtight with a twist tie—this is called the greenhouse effect. Refrigerate—right side up, please. If you are going to use the parsley within a few hours, wash, shake dry, and refrigerate wrapped in paper towels. The greenhouse treatment works equally well with flat-leaf parsley, cilantro (fresh coriander or Chinese parsley), and watercress.

It's Spreadable and Stuffable! (page 13). Photo courtesy of
Thomas J. Lipton, Inc.

Carrot-Turkey-Spinach Pâté

Makes 2 loaves (16 servings)
  Carrot Layer (recipe follows)
  Turkey Layer (recipe follows)
  Spinach Layer (recipe follows)
  Butter
  Fresh carrots, finely shredded (optional)
  Lettuce greens (optional)

Butter two 8½x4½-inch loaf pans. Line bottom
and long sides of each with foil; butter foil. Prepare
Carrot Layer and divide mixture between loaf pans.
Wash and dry processor container. Next, prepare Turkey Layer. Spoon small dollops of turkey mixture over
Carrot Layer in pans. Carefully spread turkey mixture
to form an even layer without disturbing the carrot
layer. Wash and dry processor container. Now prepare
Spinach Layer.

Spread spinach mixture carefully over Turkey Layer in
pans. Cover pans with wax paper, then aluminum foil.
Set both pans into a 13x9x2-inch baking or small roasting pan. Place on oven shelf. Pour boiling water into
roasting pan to a depth of 1 inch. Bake loaves in a
preheated 350°F. oven or until pâté feels firm to the
touch. Transfer loaf pans to a wire rack. Cool 1 hour.
Refrigerate overnight. Loosen pâté around sides of pan;
invert onto a rectangular place, unmold, peel off foil.
With small spatula or knife, smooth out surfaces. If
desired, coat the sides of pâté with finely shredded fresh
carrots. Return pâté to refrigerator until serving time.
Cut into slices for serving. Serve on a bed of lettuce or
greens.

Carrot Layer

  2 cans (16 ounces each) sliced carrots, drained
  1 cup Smucker's Low Sugar Orange Marmalade
  2 large eggs
  ¼ cup all-purpose flour
  ½ teaspoon salt
  ¼ teaspoon ground nutmeg

Place carrot slices on paper towels to drain; pat dry.
In a food processor container, place carrots, orange
marmalade, eggs, flour, salt, and nutmeg. Cover and
process until smooth.

Turkey Layer

  1 medium onion, cut into chunks
  1½ pounds ground uncooked turkey
  ⅔ cups packaged bread crumbs
  2 teaspoons poultry seasoning or crumbled sage
  1½ teaspoons salt
  ¼ teaspoon ground white pepper
  2 large eggs

In food processor container, place onion chunks, cover
and process until chopped. Remove half of the chopped
onion and reserve for the Spinach layer. Add turkey,
bread crumbs, seasoning, salt, pepper, and eggs to onion
in container. Cover and process until well mixed.

Spinach Layer

  2 packages (10 ounces each) frozen chopped
      spinach, thawed Onion (reserved from Turkey
      Layer)
  2 large eggs
  ¼ cup grated fresh Parmesan cheese
  ¼ cup packaged bread crumbs

Drain spinach, 1 package at a time, in a sieve or
strainer. With hands, squeeze spinach to wring out all
moisture. Place spinach in processor container. Add reserved onion, eggs, cheese, and bread crumbs. Cover
and process until well mixed and spinach is finely
chopped.

Anchovy and Sweet Pepper

Makes 8 servings
  1 can flat anchovies
  2 sweet red peppers (pimientos)
  8 tablespoons Filippo Berio Olive Oil
  1½ tablespoons Filippo Berio Wine Vinegar
      Melba crackers

Cut pimiento into slices about ½ inch wide and 3 inches long. Remove anchovies from can and drain off the oil. Placed 1 anchovy fillet on each strip of pimiento, rolling them together and piercing with a toothpick to hold them firm. Place them in a serving dish. Mix the olive oil and wine vinegar thoroughly and pour over the pimiento and anchovy rolls. Serve with melba crackers.

Mushroom Pâté

Makes 12 to 14 servings
    1 pound fresh mushrooms
    ¼ cup butter or margarine
    ⅓ cup minced onion
    ⅓ cup finely chopped celery
    2 eggs
    1 package (3 ounces) cream cheese, softened
    ¾ cup fine dry bread crumbs
    1 teaspoon salt
    ½ teaspoon basil leaves, crushed
    ¼ teaspoon rosemary leaves, crushed
    ¼ teaspoon oregano leaves, crushed
    ⅛ teaspoon ground black pepper
        Crackers
        Mushroom slices, grated carrots, chopped
            onion (optional)

Preheat oven to 400°F. Rinse, pat dry, and finely chop mushrooms (makes about 5 cups); set aside. In a large saucepan, melt butter. Add onion and celery; sauté until tender, about 5 minutes; set aside. In a large mixing bowl, beat eggs and cream cheese until smooth. Add bread crumbs, salt, basil, rosemary, oregano, black pepper and reserved onion and celery mixture and mushrooms. Stir until mixture is well blended and smooth. Butter a 7x4x2-inch loaf pan. Cover the long sides and bottom of pan with a strip of waxed paper leaving a 1½-inch overhang. Spoon mushroom mixture evenly into pan. Cover top of pan

Baba Ghanoush. Caloric Corporation

with foil. Bake until firm, about 1½ hours. Cool in pan until lukewarm. Remove from pan using waxed paper overhang as an aid; discard paper. Serve at room temperature with crackers, as an appetizer garnished with mushroom slices, grated carrot, and chopped onion, if desired.

Caponata

Makes 8 to 10 servings
    1 medium eggplant
    6 tablespoons Filippo Berio Olive Oil
    1 onion, sliced
    3 tablespoons tomato sauce
    2 stalks celery, diced
    2 tablespoons Filippo Berio Wine Vinegar
    1 tablespoon sugar
    1 tablespoon capers, drained
    4 green olives, stuffed with red peppers, chopped
    ¼ teaspoon salt
    ⅛ teaspoon pepper
        Toasted bread

Peel and dice eggplant; sauté in 5 tablespoons olive oil. Remove eggplant from pan, add 1 additional tablespoon of olive oil. Fry onions until brown. Add tomato sauce and celery; cook until celery is tender. If needed, add tablespoon of water. Return eggplant to pan; add capers and chopped olives. Heat wine vinegar with sugar and pour over eggplant. Add salt and pepper to taste. Simmer for 10 to 15 minutes, stirring frequently. Serve cool on toasted squares of bread. Leftovers can be put into refrigerator for later use.

Baba Ghanoush

Makes 8 to 10 servings
    1 1¼-pound eggplant
    ½ teaspoon salt
    1 clove garlic, or to taste
    3 teaspoons lemon juice
    2 tablespoons olive oil
        Fresh bread crumbs (optional)
        Sliced ripe olives (optional)
        Warm pita bread, cut into wedges

Rinse eggplant and pat dry. Pierce in several places with sharp knife. Place in baking dish. Bake at 350°F. 45 to 50 minutes until very soft. Cool until easy to handle. Cut in half and scoop out pulp. Place pulp in food processor or blender. Add salt, garlic, and lemon juice. Purée until smooth. Blend in oil until well mixed. If too thin, add 2 or 3 tablespoons bread crumbs and mix well. Spoon back into shell; garnish with olives, if desired. Serve as dip with pita bread.

Skinny Eggplant Dip

Makes 2½ cups

1 large eggplant (1 to 1¼ pounds)
1 large garlic, crushed
1 cup Colombo Original Plain Yogurt
1 teaspoon salt
1 teaspoon red pepper
2 tablespoons parsley, minced

With a fork, prick the eggplant 2 or 3 times. Place on a cookie sheet in 325°F. oven and bake 1 hour, or until very soft. Let eggplant cool a little, scoop out all the pulp, and mash well. Add all other ingredients and chill.

Skinny Crimson Dip

Makes 2¾ cups

½ cup red pepper relish
3 cups Colombo Original Plain Yogurt
  Red and green peppers

Drain relish for 1 hour. Mix together with yogurt, blend well. Chill. Cut red and green peppers into strips and serve with dip.

Confetti Dip

Makes 10 servings

1 package (8 ounces) cream cheese
½ cup sour cream
2 tablespoons snipped parsley
2 tablespoons chopped radishes
2 tablespoons snipped chives
2 tablespoons chopped celery
1 teaspoon white pepper
1 tablespoon chopped dill
  Assorted crûdités

Mix cream cheese and sour cream together until smooth. Save about 2 tablespoons of chopped vegetables for garnish; mix rest into cheese mixture, along with dill and pepper. Refrigerate at least 1 hour before serving. Right before serving, sprinkle reserved vegetables over dip; serve with crûdités.

Olive Vegetable Antipasto

Makes about 5 cups

1 jar (9¾ ounces) olive condite, undrained
2 cups thinly sliced cucumbers
2 cups thinly sliced celery
2 cups thinly sliced carrots
¼ cup chopped parsley

In a large bowl, thoroughly combine all ingredients. Place in a container with a tight-fitting lid. Chill thoroughly.

Raisin-Carrot Spread

Makes about 1½ cups

¼ cup mayonnaise
½ cup creamed cottage cheese
  Dash salt
  Dash hot pepper sauce
½ cup seedless raisins
1 large carrot, pared and cut up

Put mayonnaise, cottage cheese, salt, and hot pepper sauce into blender container. Cover; blend at high speed until smooth. Add raisins and carrot. Cover; blend at medium speed just until raisins and carrot are chopped.

Skinny Jade Dip

Makes about 1 cup dip

1 cup watercress, loosely packed
1 cup parsley, loosely packed
1 cup Colombo Original Plain Yogurt
1 tablespoon minced green onions
1 clove garlic, minced
1 teaspoon salt
  Carrot and celery sticks
  Thin slices roast chicken or turkey

Wash watercress and parsley well. Dry and remove heavy stems. Mince very fine with knife or use a food processor. (Add 2 tablespoons yogurt if using a food processor.) In a small bowl, fold watercress-parsley mixture into yogurt. Stir in green onions, garlic, and salt. Chill. Serve with carrot and celery sticks and thin slices of chicken or turkey.

Crab-Stuffed Cherry Tomatoes

Makes about 20 appetizers

1 pint cherry tomatoes
1 package (6 ounces) frozen crabmeat, thawed, drained on paper towels
¼ cup Hellmann's or Best Foods Real Mayonnaise
¾ teaspoon grated lemon rind
½ teaspoon curry powder
¼ teaspoon salt

Thinly slice tops and bottoms from tomatoes. Remove pulp from stem end; drain. In medium bowl, stir together crab, mayonnaise, lemon rind, curry powder, and salt until well blended. Fill tomatoes with crab mixture. Cover; refrigerate until ready to serve.

Marinated Mushrooms

Makes 8 to 10 servings

    2 quarts water
    2 pounds fresh medium mushrooms
    2 teaspoons lemon juice
    ¾ cup Wish-Bone® Italian Dressing

In large saucepan, bring water to a boil. Add mushrooms and lemon juice and cook 2 minutes; drain. Toss with Wish-Bone Italian Dressing; cover and marinate in refrigerator 4 hours or overnight, turning occasionally. Serve with cold meats or poultry or as an hors d'oeuvre.

Mushrooms à la Grecque

Makes 6½ cups

    2 cups chicken broth
    ⅔ cup dry white wine
    ⅔ cup olive oil
    ¼ cup lemon juice
    2½ teaspoons salt
    1 teaspoon thyme leaves, crushed
    ½ teaspoon fennel seed, crushed
    2 cloves garlic, minced
    1½ pounds fresh mushrooms
    1 cup sliced zucchini
    ⅔ cup diced green pepper
    ½ cup sliced carrot

In large skillet, combine chicken broth, wine, olive oil, lemon juice, salt, thyme, fennel, and garlic; bring to a boil. Reduce heat and simmer covered 15 minutes. Meanwhile, rinse, pat dry and trim mushrooms (cut in halves if large). Place mushrooms in simmering marinade; simmer, covered, until lightly cooked, about 4 minutes. Remove with a slotted spoon to a medium bowl. Repeat separately (to retain color) with zucchini (about 1½ minutes), green pepper (about 1 minute), and carrot (about 3 minutes). Pour marinade over vegetables. Cover and refrigerate overnight. Serve as an appetizer, hors d'oeuvre, a meat accompaniment, or in tossed salads.

Hot Mushroom Caps

Makes 1 dozen

    ½ pound mushrooms
    2 tablespoons melted butter
    1 medium-size onion, finely chopped
    2 tablespoons butter
    ½ cup chopped stuffed olives
    1 tablespoon dry sherry

Wash mushrooms, pat dry, and carefully remove stems. Brush caps with 2 tablespoons butter. Place in a very shallow baking pan and broil, 4 inches from the source of the heat, about 5 minutes, or until lightly browned. Meanwhile, chop mushroom stems. Cook stems and onion in 2 tablespoons butter in a skillet until lightly browned. Add olives and sherry. Mix well. Fill mushroom caps with olive mixture. Broil 3 to 4 inches from source of heat for 5 minutes, or until filling is lightly browned.

Versatile Vegetable Appetizer

Compose a platter of crûdités—fresh raw vegetables cut into pieces of a size easy to handle—keeping in mind color, texture, and taste, and set a bowl of accompanying dip on the platter or close by. Plain yogurt, seasoned with chives, curry powder, chili powder, chopped dill (or dill pickle), or parsley or tarragon makes a most acceptable dip for crûdités. Divide a round wooden tray into wedge-shaped sixths with whole scallions. In each of the spaces between, heap sliced raw cauliflower, sliced radishes, carrot strips, cucumber fingers with the peel left on, zucchini rounds, and strips of white turnip. Or compose the vegetables—any combination you like (additional suggestions are little green onions, small button mushrooms, strips of green pepper, young broccoli flowerets, or tender green beans)—in concentric circles around the bowl of dip, or put the dip to one side of the platter or tray and arrange the vegetables in diagonal strips. Raw vegetables may also be cut and shaped to be served on their own or to be used as a garnish for other appetizers. Dress up small pickles this way: Using a sharp knife, cut them into thin lengthwise slices, starting ⅛ of an inch from the stem end; then gently spread the slices apart to form a fan.

Whatever you choose to offer as an appetizer, there is a way—usually several ways—to dress it up. Garnishing takes only a moment of planning when you decide on your menu, a few moments of doing before you serve, and crûdités can be prepared as long as 24 hours in advance and refrigerated until serving time.

Spinach Dip (page 13). Seven Seas®/Phil Kretchmar

Skinny Crimson Dip (page 16). Courtesy of Colombo, Inc.

Confetti Dip (page 16)

Skinny Jade Dip (page 16). Courtesy of Colombo, Inc.

Cheese-Mushroom Roll-Ups

Makes 24 appetizers

     1 tablespoon butter or margarine
     ½ pound mushrooms, minced
     ¼ teaspoon fines herbes or thyme
     ¼ teaspoon salt
     2 tablespoons cornstarch
     2 tablespoons dry white wine
    1½ ounces cream cheese (½ 3-ounce package)
     1 sheet frozen puff pastry (½ 17½-ounce
         package), thawed
     1 egg yolk, beaten

In a medium skillet, melt butter. Add mushrooms, fines herbes, and salt and sauté until very tender. Blend cornstarch and wine and stir into mushroom mixture; cook until thickened. Cut cream cheese into chunks and stir into mushroom mixture until smooth. Chill mixture well. Place cold puff pastry on lightly floured surface. Cut pastry in half lengthwise. Spread chilled mushroom mixture on each piece of pastry to within ¼ inch of one long edge. Brush edge with some of the egg yolk. Roll up starting from opposite long edge. Press seam to seal. Place rolled pastry on plate and freeze 20 minutes, or until firm. Brush rolls with remaining egg yolk; cut each roll into 12 pieces. Place rolls, cut side down, on lightly greased baking sheet.

Preheat oven to 350°F. Bake 18 to 20 minutes until lightly browned and flaky. Cool slightly before removing from baking sheet.

Broiled Stuffed Mushrooms

Makes 12 stuffed mushrooms
    1½ **slices bread**
    ½ **cup cubed cooked ham**
    12 **large mushrooms**
    1 **small onion, cut up**
    3 **tablespoons butter or margarine**
    2 **tablespoons light cream**
    1 **teaspoon prepared mustard**
    ¼ **teaspoon Worcestershire sauce**
    ¼ **teaspoon pepper**

Heat broiler. Tear bread slices into blender container. Cover; blend at medium speed until crumbled; empty onto wax paper. Put ham into blender container. Cover; blend at medium speed until chopped; empty onto wax paper. Wipe mushrooms with damp cloth. Remove stems; set caps aside. Put mushroom stems and onion into blender container. Cover; blend at medium speed until chopped. Heat 1 tablespoon butter in skillet. Add mushroom-onion mixture; cook over medium heat, stirring occasionally, until onion is transparent. Stir in cream, mustard, Worcestershire, and pepper. Stir in bread crumbs and ham. Place mushroom caps on baking sheet, cavity sides down. Melt remaining 2 tablespoons butter; brush mushroom caps lightly. Broil 2 minutes. Invert mushroom caps; fill with ham stuffing; brush with remaining melted butter. Broil 3 minutes or until lightly browned.

Broiled Stuffed Mushrooms. Hamilton Beach Scovill Inc.

Cheesey Celery Snack

Makes 2½ cups
    ½ **pound grated Cheez-Ola®**
    ¼ **cup finely chopped ripe olives**
    2 **tablespoons chopped green pepper**
       Dash garlic powder
    ½ **cup safflower mayonnaise**
       Celery stalks
       Crackers or bread

Combine all ingredients except crackers or bread in medium-size bowl. Use mixture to stuff celery stalks, or serve on crackers or bread.

Zippy Potato Skins

Makes 12 appetizer servings
    6 **large baking potatoes**
    ¼ **cup butter or margarine, melted**
    6 **tablespoons Durkee RedHot! Sauce**
    ½ **cup (4 ounces) shredded Monterey Jack cheese**
       Crisp-fried crumbled bacon (optional)

Bake potatoes at 400°F. for 1 hour, or until done. Combine melted butter and hot sauce; set aside. Halve each potato lengthwise; scoop out pulp leaving ¼-inch shell. Cut each shell in lengthwise strips 1 inch wide. Place strips on broiler pan; broil 3 to 4 inches from the heat until crisp, about 5 minutes. (Or place strips on baking sheet; bake at 450°F. for 12 to 15 minutes, or until crisp.) Brush skins with hot sauce mixture; top with shredded cheese. Return to broiler for 1 minute, or until cheese melts (or return to oven for 4 to 5 minutes). Sprinkle with bacon, if desired.

Tasty 'Tater Tidbits

Makes 18 appetizers
    6 **slices Armour Star Bologna, cut in thirds**
    18 **frozen shredded potato rounds, thawed**
    ¼ **cup barbecue sauce**

Heat oven to 400°F. Wrap bologna piece around each potato round. Thread bologna-potato rounds on skewers; brush with barbecue sauce. Bake at 400°F. for 10 minutes.

New Ways with Parsley

Creamed Parsley is a delicious vegetable. Discard the heavy stems from 2 pounds of parsley to serve 4 people. Wash, cook briefly until just wilted, and drain well. Mix with a white sauce made with ½ cup chopped shallots briefly sautéed in ½ cup butter or margarine, thickened with ¼ cup all-purpose flour; use 1 cup heavy cream and 1 cup milk, or 2 cups half and half, as the liquid, and season with salt and white pepper. *Fried Parsley* is delicious as an appetizer or snack food, or as the green in a meat or cheese sandwich. Heat 1 inch oil to 370°F. in a deep pan. Discard stems of ¼ pound washed parsley; pat parsley dry with paper towels. Fry by the handful in hot oil (be careful, it splatters), just until the parsley turns bright green, about 3 seconds. Lift out with a slotted spoon and drain on paper towels. *Fresh Parsley Relish* is great with cold lamb or chicken, and it makes an excellent dip, as well as a dressing for cold cooked vegetable salads. In the blender container, combine 2 cups washed parsley (pack to measure), ½ cup mint leaves, 2 teaspoons chopped fresh ginger, 5 peeled cloves garlic, 2 tablespoons lemon juice, ¾ cup unflavored yogurt, and a dash of hot pepper sauce. Process until puréed. Store covered in the refrigerator.

Potato Chips

Makes 4 quarts
- 8 **large potatoes, washed and peeled**
- **Ice water**
- **Peanut or corn oil for deep-fat frying**
- **Salt (optional)**

Slice potatoes paper-thin (approximately ¹⁄₁₆ inch) with a vegetable peeler or sharp knife. Soak slices in ice water for 2 hours. Heat oil in deep-fat fryer (or 4 inches oil in large deep saucepan) to 380°F. Drain potato slices; dry thoroughly on paper towels. Place separated slices in fry basket. Lower into oil. Shake basket or stir several times to prevent slices from sticking together. Deep-fat fry until golden. Remove from oil. Drain well on paper towels. Sprinkle with salt, if desired. Cool before serving. Store in airtight container.

Nacho Rounds

Makes 5 to 6 servings
- 1 **large potato, washed and unpeeled**
- 2 **tablespoons hot taco sauce**
- 1 **can (4 ounces) chopped mild or hot green chilies, drained**
- ¾ **cup shredded cheddar cheese**

Preheat oven to 350°F. Cut potato vertically into 20 slices. Place in single layer on greased baking sheet. Brush each slice with taco sauce. Sprinkle with chilies and cheese. Bake 25 minutes, or until potatoes are tender and cheese is golden brown. Serve warm.

Yam Chips

Makes 8 servings
- 6 **yams**
- **Salt**
- **Oil or shortening for deep-fat frying**

Peel yams and slice as thinly as you can—as if you were making potato chips. Soak for 3 hours in cold salted water. Drain well and pat dry with paper towels. Drop a few at a time in deep fat heated to 400°F. and cook until golden brown. Drain thoroughly. Sprinkle with salt while hot.

Uniformity Is Not a Dirty Word

When you're preparing vegetables for a special-occasion meal, take the few extra minutes it requires to make them into uniform shapes. Cut potatoes, turnips, or rutabagas into neat balls with the large end of a melon baller, or trim them with a sharp knife into large olive shapes. Cook them until they are barely tender, drain them well, and sauté them briefly in butter. (If you like, add a little sugar to the butter, in the Danish manner, for a browner, tastier glaze.) When you buy asparagus, make sure that the stalks are uniform in diameter; when you prepare it, make sure that they're uniform in length. Buy baby carrots, and trim them to uniform size and shape. (Glaze these in butter/sugar—brown or white—if a sweet touch is appropriate to the rest of the meal.) Sauté uniform-size cherry tomatoes briefly for a glowing red color. Any of these shapely vegetables makes an attractive edible border garnish for a platter of meat, fish, or poultry. And you're not being wasteful—cook the trimmings and mash or purée them for another meal, or use them in soup.

Fried Potato Logs

Makes 28 appetizers

    2 cups mashed potatoes, chilled
    1 egg yolk
    1 tablespoon onion flakes
    ⅓ cup all-purpose flour
    1 egg
    ½ cup dry bread crumbs
    5 tablespoons vegetable shortening

Combine potatoes, egg yolk, and onion flakes in medium bowl; blend well. Shape mixture into 28 logs about 2½ inches long. Roll logs in flour to coat. Combine egg and 2 tablespoons water in small bowl; mix lightly. Dip logs in egg, then into bread crumbs. Melt shortening in large skillet on moderate heat. Fry logs, 8 at a time, until golden brown, turning to brown all sides. Cool slightly before serving.

Potato Cheese Balls

Makes 28 to 30 appetizers

    2 cups mashed potatoes, chilled
    ½ cup grated process American cheese
    1 egg
    1 tablespoon milk
    ½ cup dry bread crumbs

Combine potatoes and cheese in medium bowl; blend well. Shape mixture into 28 to 30 balls. In separate bowl, whisk together egg and milk. Dip balls in egg, then roll in bread crumbs. Place balls on baking sheet. Broil, 5 inches from heat, 4 to 6 minutes, or until golden brown. Turn and brown other side, about 4 minutes. Serve warm on wooden toothpicks.

Hawaiian Tidbits

Makes 18 appetizers

    2 Italian sausages, casings removed, cut into 18
        slices
    1 large potato, washed, peeled, and cut into 18
        cubes
    1 can (5¼ ounces) pineapple chunks, drained
    2 tablespoons teriyaki sauce

Preheat oven to 375°F. Using wooden skewers, alternate 1 piece sausage, 1 cube potato, and 1 chunk pineapple on each skewer. Lay each kebab on lightly greased baking sheet. Brush with teriyaki sauce. Bake 20 to 25 minutes, or until sausage is cooked and potatoes are tender. Turn several times during cooking. Serve hot.

Potato Puffs

Makes 4 servings

        Peanut or corn oil for deep-fat frying
    ½ cup all-purpose flour
    1 teaspoon baking powder
    ¼ teaspoon salt
    1 cup mashed potatoes
    1 egg, lightly beaten
    1 teaspoon minced parsley
        Salt (optional)

Heat oil in deep-fat fryer (or 4 inches oil in large deep saucepan) to 385°F. Combine flour, baking powder, and salt in medium bowl. Add potatoes; blend thoroughly. Add egg and parsley; blend well. Drop potato mixture by teaspoonfuls into hot oil. Deep-fat fry until golden brown. Remove with slotted spoon. Drain on paper towels. Sprinkle with salt, if desired.

Potato Appetizers

Chips are not the be-all and end-all of potatoes when snacking is in order. Cut unpeeled medium baking potatoes into 8 wedges each. Dip in melted butter, coating well, and place on baking sheet cut side down. Bake in preheated 375°F. oven 30 minutes; turn over and bake 25 minutes longer, or until golden and edges are crisp. Serve at once, with dipping sauces. Unflavored yogurt mixed with a generous amount of thinly sliced green onion makes a good sauce for these. So does cheddar cheese melted with a little milk, onion powder, and prepared mustard. So does half and half, catsup, and sour cream seasoned liberally with chili powder, or mayonnaise and plain yogurt in the same proportions, seasoned with a squirt of lemon juice and plenty of curry powder.

Vegetable Beer Batter

Makes 2 cups

    1 cup all-purpose flour
    1 tablespoon cornstarch
    1 egg yolk
    ½ teaspoon salt
    12 ounces Lowenbrau beer

Combine ingredients in mixer or whisk by hand to blend. There may be small lumps. Keep mixture refrigerated until ready to use. Use for batter-fried artichoke hearts, green pepper rings, onion rings, mushrooms, carrot sticks, zucchini sticks, etc. Dip vegetables in batter, deep-fry in 375°F. oil until light golden in color, 2 to 3 minutes. Drain on paper towels.

Potato Chips (page 20); Hash Browns (page 114); French Fries (page 111); Basic Twice-Baked Potatoes (page 112). Wisconsin Potato Growers Auxiliary

Antipasto Appetizer Tray

Makes 20 servings

> 1 package (10 ounces) frozen asparagus, cooked according to package directions
> 1 package (10 ounces) frozen cauliflower, partially cooked, cut into flowerets
> 1 can (6 ounces) pitted ripe olives, drained
> 1 cucumber, thinly sliced
> 1 cup cherry tomato halves
> ½ pound mushrooms, sliced
> 1 bottle (8 ounces) Italian salad dressing
> 1 package (4 ounces) Armour Star Genoa Salami
> 1 package (4 ounces) Armour Star Tangy Beef Thuringer
> 1 package (6 ounces) sliced provolone cheese, cut in quarters
> Lettuce leaves
> Carrot strips

Place vegetables in separate containers; pour dressing over vegetables. Cover; marinate in refrigerator overnight. Arrange vegetables, sausages and cheese on lettuce-covered platter. Garnish with carrot.

Artichoke Devils

Makes 8 servings

> 8 hard-cooked eggs
> 1½ to 2 tablespoons whipped sweet butter
> 1 teaspoon onion juice
> Salt and white pepper to taste
> 1 package (9 ounces) frozen artichoke hearts
> ¼ cup wine vinegar
> ¼ cup olive oil
> 1 teaspoon salt
> ¼ teaspoon freshly ground black pepper
> Paprika

As soon as eggs are cool enough to handle, shell them, cut in halves lengthwise, and turn yolks into a small bowl. With a fork, mash thoroughly. Add enough butter to make a thick paste, remembering that the paste will thicken after the eggs are refrigerated. Add onion juice and salt and pepper to taste. Fill whites; cover and refrigerate. Cook artichoke hearts according to package directions. Cut each in half lengthwise. Combine vinegar, oil, salt, and pepper and marinate artichoke pieces in this liquid overnight. To serve, drain artichokes and place one on the yolk of each deviled egg; sprinkle with paprika.

Antipasto Appetizer Tray. Armour Food Company

Londonderry Watercress Rounds

Makes 60 appetizers
  ½ cup butter or margarine, softened
  ¼ cup Wish-Bone® Creamy Cucumber Dressing
  1 cup chopped watercress
  30 slices thin-sliced white bread

In small bowl, blend butter and Wish-Bone Creamy Cucumber Dressing; add watercress. Using 1½-inch biscuit cutter, cut 120 rounds from bread. Cut ½-inch circle from center of half the round to form "doughnut" shape. Spread remaining rounds with dressing mixture, then top with "doughnut" rounds. Wrap in waxed paper or plastic wrap and chill. Garnish, if desired, with sprig of watercress in center of each.

Gold-and-Emerald Ribbon Sandwiches

Makes 30 sandwiches
  2 hard-cooked eggs, shelled
    Mayonnaise
  3 tablespoons chopped, raw spinach leaves
    Pinch of salt
  1 small ripe avocado
  1 teaspoon lemon juice
  12 slices white sandwich bread
  6 slices whole wheat bread

Mash eggs very well. Combine with ¼ cup mayonnaise, spinach leaves, and salt. Peel avocado; pit and press through a sieve. Stir in lemon juice. Trim crust from white and whole wheat bread slices. Spread white bread with mayonnaise. On 6 slices spread egg mixture. Spread whole wheat bread with avocado mixture. Place avocado layer on top of egg layer. Top with remaining white slices, mayonnaise side down. Wrap in waxed paper and chill. Before serving, cut each sandwich into 5 ribbon slices.

Banderillas

Makes about 20 appetizers
  1 pound shrimp (about 20), cleaned and cooked
  2 cans (14 ounces each) artichoke hearts, drained and halved, or 2 packages (9 ounces each) frozen artichoke hearts, cooked and drained
  ¾ cup Wish-Bone® Italian Dressing
  ¼ cup finely chopped parsley

In shallow dish, combine all ingredients. Cover and marinate in refrigerator, turning occasionally, 4 hours or overnight. To serve, skewer shrimp and artichokes on wooden skewers or toothpicks.

Huevos à la Española

Makes about 35 appetizers
  ½ cup Wish-Bone® Italian Dressing
  1 can (16 ounces) whole tomatoes, chopped and drained
  ½ cup finely chopped green pepper
  ½ cup finely chopped onion
  8 eggs
  2 tablespoons finely chopped parsley
  ¼ pound chorizo or pepperoni, cut into ¼-inch slices

Preheat oven to 400°F. In 15x10x1-inch jelly roll pan, combine ¼ cup Wish-Bone Italian Dressing, tomatoes, green pepper, and onion. Bake 15 minutes; remove from oven and spread mixture evenly over pan. Add eggs beaten with remaining dressing and parsley; top with sausage in checkerboard fashion. Bake an additional 10 minutes or until set. To serve, cut into 2-inch squares.

Beef and Mushroom Turnovers

Makes 24 turnovers
  1 pound ground beef
  ¼ cup chopped onion
  1 envelope Lipton® Beef Flavor Mushroom Recipe Soup Mix
  1 cup shredded cheddar cheese
  ¼ cup sliced pimiento-stuffed olives
  3 packages (8 ounces each) refrigerated crescent rolls

Preheat oven to 375°F. In medium skillet, brown ground beef and onion; blend in Lipton Beef Flavor Mushroom Recipe Soup Mix, cheese, and olives. Separate dough according to package directions. Place spoonful of meat mixture in center of each triangle; fold over and seal edges tightly with fork. Place on ungreased cookie sheet and bake 15 minutes or until golden brown.

Decorative Vegetable Holders

Savory mixtures profit by being served in decorative vegetable holders rather than on bread or crackers. Blades of Belgian endive, whole inner ribs or chunks of larger ribs of celery or of fennel, raw mushroom caps, hollowed-out cherry tomatoes, little cups made of beets or carrots, or zucchini (raw or cooked)—all serve well to hold smooth fillings, bland or sharp, and to add flavor and texture. For cooked vegetables, choose small beets, leaving them whole, and cut 2-inch-long chunks from unpeeled zucchini or scraped carrots; cook them separately in boiling salted water only until they are tender. Use a ball cutter or a sharp, pointed knife to make a hollow for the filling, being sure to leave sufficient vegetable, bottom and sides, so that the cups won't fall apart.

Tuck a whole almond or a tiny pickled onion into the top of the filling, or sprinkle chopped peanuts, walnuts, pecans, or pistachios, snipped chives or mint, or chopped capers on stuffed celery or endive, and you've added another dimension of appeal to both sight and taste.

Dill pickles are very good additions to a tray of appetizers, but, face it, a dill pickle is rather homely, and cutting it into slices or wedges doesn't improve it perceptibly. Ah, but hollow it (use an apple corer), stuff it with a mixture of cream cheese and tiny bits of smoked salmon, chill it thoroughly, cut it into ¼-inch-thick slices, and you have a garnish worth looking at—and worth eating.

Marinated Vegetable Kebabs, Italiano

Makes about 30 kebabs

- 1 jar (3¾ ounces) marinated mushrooms, undrained
- 1 medium-size green pepper, cut into squares
- 15 cherry tomatoes (about), halved
- ½ teaspoon salt
- 1 lemon

In a medium bowl, combine all ingredients except lemon; mix well. Cover and refrigerate 2 to 3 hours. On short skewers or toothpicks, place a mushroom, a tomato half, and a green pepper square. To serve, cut a thin slice from a lemon so that it stands in place. Poke kebabs in lemon.

Brunch Kebabs

Makes 2 servings

- 4 slices raw bacon
- 8 mushrooms
- 8 cherry tomatoes
- 8 chunks green pepper

Cut bacon into squares. Wipe off mushrooms with a damp paper towel. Wash tomatoes and dry. Thread on 4 short skewers in this manner: bacon, tomato, bacon, pepper, bacon, mushrooms—repeat. Broil until bacon is crisp, turning frequently.

A Little Bit of Italy

Makes 20 servings

- 4 envelopes Knox Unflavored Gelatine
- 3½ cups cold water, divided
- 2 cups boiling water
- 1½ cups Wish-Bone® Italian Dressing
- 1½ cups chopped green pepper
- ½ cup sliced pitted ripe olives
- ⅓ cup diced pimiento
- 1 can (7 ounces) tuna, drained and flaked
- 1 can (4 ounces) sliced mushrooms, drained
- Lettuce leaves
- Ripe olives (optional)
- Salami (optional)
- Provolone cheese (optional)

In a large bowl, mix Knox Unflavored Gelatine and ½ cup cold water. Add 2 cups boiling water and stir until gelatine is completely dissolved. Add remaining 3 cups cold water and Wish-Bone Italian Dressing; chill, stirring occasionally, until mixture is the consistency of unbeaten egg whites. Fold in green pepper, olives, pimiento, tuna, and mushrooms. Turn into a 13x9x2-inch pan or individual molds and chill until firm. To serve, cut into squares and place each serving on a lettuce leaf. Garnish with ripe olives, salami, and provolone cheese, if desired.

Bright Beginnings

Sit-down first courses, fork-and-plate appetizers that range all the way from light to hearty, and all of them vegetable based.

Stuffed Fresh Artichokes

Makes 4 servings
- **4 large fresh whole artichokes**
- **1 cup chopped fresh mushrooms**
- **¼ cup chopped shallots or white onions**
- **1 tablespoon chopped chervil**
- **1 tablespoon chopped chives**
- **1 can (10½ ounces) Campbell's Condensed Cream of Mushroom Soup**
- **1 tablespoon liquid meat extract**
- **¼ cup grated Parmesan cheese**
  Paprika

Trim the spiny points from the artichoke leaves, using a pair of shears. Parboil. Combine mushrooms, shallots, chervil, chives, mushroom soup, and liquid meat extract. Stuff the mushroom mixture between the leaves and over the tops of the artichokes. Place artichokes in a shallow baking pan. Sprinkle with grated Parmesan cheese and paprika. Bake in a preheated 350°F. oven for 40 to 45 minutes, or until an artichoke is easily pierced through to the bottom.

Artichokes with Lamb Stuffing

Makes 4 servings
- **4 whole fresh artichokes**
- **2 tablespoons white vinegar**
- **1 pound ground lamb**
- **¾ cup chopped onion**
- **2 tablespoons cooking oil**
- **½ cup fine dry bread crumbs**
- **¼ cup snipped parsley**
- **2 eggs, beaten**
- **¼ teaspoon ground cinnamon**
- **½ teaspoon salt**
  Avgolemono Sauce (recipe follows)

Wash artichokes. Cut off stems evenly, close to the base. Cook in boiling salted water with white vinegar 25 to 30 minutes, or until a leaf can be readily pulled off. Drain upside down on paper towels. Using kitchen scissors, cut off spiny top part of each leaf. Using a teaspoon, remove small center leaves and choke—the thistlelike part at the inner base of the artichoke. Brown lamb and onion in hot oil. Drain. Add crumbs, parsley, eggs, cinnamon, and salt. Mix well. Spread artichoke leaves slightly and stuff with lamb mixture. Place in 9x9x2-inch pan and pour in 1 inch of hot water. Bake in preheated 375°F. oven for 25 to 30 minutes. Serve with Avgolemono Sauce.

Helpful to know: You can prepare and stuff the artichokes in advance; bake just before serving, extending baking time 10 minutes.

Avgolemono Sauce

Makes 4 servings
- **2 cups chicken bouillon**
- **3 eggs**
- **3 tablespoons lemon juice**

Pour bouillon into saucepan. In a bowl, beat eggs with lemon juice. Heat bouillon and add ½ cup of it slowly to eggs, beating constantly. Return eggs to remaining bouillon, stirring constanlty. Heat, but do not boil. Serve at once.

Artichokes à la King

Makes 12 appetizers
- **12 canned or frozen artichoke bottoms, drained**
- **1 can (4 ounces) crabmeat, drained**
- **1 tablespoon fresh parsley, chopped**
- **1 tablespoon celery, chopped**
- **1 clove garlic, minced**
  Juice of ½ lemon
- **1 tablespoon mayonnaise**
  Salt and pepper to taste
- **¼ cup Paul Masson Chablis**
  Lemon slices

Mix all ingredients except artichoke bottoms, then stuff artichokes with mixture. Chill for ½ hour before serving. Cut lemon slices in quarters and garnish.

Cranberry Waldorf Mold (page 63); Acorn Squash High-Rise (page 42); Turnips au Gratin (page 44). United Fresh Fruit & Vegetable Association

Green Bean Casserole

Makes 4 to 6 servings

    1 pound fresh green beans or 2 packages (10
        ounces each) frozen cut green beans
    2 tablespoons butter
    3 tablespoons whole wheat flour
    ½ cup milk
    ½ onion, grated
    1 tablespoon Sue Bee Honey
    ⅓ teaspoon salt (optional)
    ⅛ teaspoon pepper
    1½ cups yogurt
    4 hard-cooked eggs, sliced
    ½ pound Swiss cheese, slivered or grated
    ¼ cup wheat germ
    1 tablespoon oil

Cook and drain green beans. Melt butter, add flour, and stir until blended. Add milk and continue to cook, stirring until thickened. Add grated onion, Sue Bee Honey, seasonings, and yogurt. Mix until smooth. Remove from heat. Preheat oven to 350°F. Layer green beans, hard-cooked eggs, and cheese. Pour sauce over top, poking casserole with a fork to be sure sauce seeps into all layers. Sprinkle with wheat germ mixed with a little oil. Bake for 10 to 15 minutes, or until sauce is bubbling and cheese is melted. Be careful not to overbake as eggs can become rubbery.

Holiday Green Bean Casserole

Makes 6 servings

    2 cans (1 pound each) cut green beans, drained,
        or 2 packages (9 ounces each) frozen cut
        green beans, cooked and drained
    ¾ cup milk
    1 can (10¾ ounces) condensed cream of
        mushroom soup
    ⅛ teaspoon Durkee Ground Black Pepper
    1 can (2.8 ounces) Durkee French Fried Onions

Combine beans, milk, soup, pepper, and one-half can of French Fried Onions; pour into a 1½-quart casserole. Bake uncovered at 350°F. for 30 minutes. Top with remaining onions and bake 5 minutes longer.

Soybeans in Orange Sauce

Makes 6 servings

    1 pound dried soybeans
    2 teaspoons salt
    3½ cups Florida orange juice
    ½ cup white vinegar
    ½ cup raisins
    ¼ cup molasses
    ⅓ cup chopped onion
    3 tablespoons butter or margarine
    1 teaspoon dry mustard
    1 teaspoon ground ginger
    ¼ teaspoon ground cloves
    5 cups hot cooked rice (optional)
      Fried Bananas (recipe follows) (optional)
    4 Florida oranges, peeled and sliced (optional)

Soak the soybeans overnight in water to cover by at least 4 inches. Drain, rinse, and place in a large saucepan. Add salted water to cover by at least 4 inches. Bring to a simmer and skim off foam. Simmer the beans, partly covered, for 4 to 5 hours, or until tender. Drain and combine with remaining ingredients in a 2-quart casserole. Cover and bake in 350°F. oven for 1 hour. Serve, or refrigerate and reheat when desired. To reheat, bake in 350°F. oven for 45 minutes. If desired, pour over hot cooked rice and garnish with Fried Bananas and orange slices.

Fried Bananas

    4 firm bananas, halved lengthwise and crosswise
    2 tablespoons butter or margarine

In large skillet, cook the bananas in butter for 2 minutes on each side, or until golden.

Broccoli Soufflé

Makes 4 servings

    2 tablespoons chopped green onion
    3 tablespoons butter or margarine
    3 tablespoons all-purpose flour
      Pepper to taste
    1 cup milk
    4 eggs, separated
    2 tablespoons grated Parmesan cheese
    1 package (10 ounces) frozen chopped broccoli,
        thawed
    1 can (12 ounces) SPAM® Luncheon Meat,
        cut into chunks
    ¼ teaspoon salt
    ¼ teaspoon cream of tartar

Butter bottom of 1½-quart soufflé dish. Tie an aluminum foil collar of double thickness around dish, extending 2 inches above top. In medium saucepan, sauté onions in butter until transparent; blend in flour and pepper. Stir in milk; cook and stir over medium heat until mixture thickens and boils. Beat egg yolks lightly; stir in a little of the hot mixture. Add yolks to saucepan with cheese; cook and stir over low heat until mixture thickens. Remove from heat. Place broccoli and SPAM® in food processor; use chopping blade and process until finely chopped (or finely chop by hand); stir into sauce mixture. Beat egg whites with salt and cream of tartar until stiff but not dry. Fold gently into SPAM® mixture. Pile into prepared soufflé dish. Bake in 375°F. oven 35 to 40 minutes, or until top is lightly browned and soufflé is set. Serve immediately.

Nice to know: Sauce mixture may be completed ahead of time. Heat sauce and fold in the beaten egg whites just before serving.

Stuffed Whole Cabbage with Corned Beef

Makes 6 servings

   1 **large cabbage**
   ¾ **teaspoon salt, divided**
   2 **tablespoons chopped butter or margarine**
   ½ **cup chopped fresh onion**
   ½ **cup chopped celery with leaves**
   ¼ **cup chopped fresh parsley**
   2 **cups finely chopped cooked corned beef**
   2 **cups diced cooked potatoes**
   ¼ **teaspoon pepper**
   1 **teaspoon caraway seed**

Remove outside leaves from cabbage. Place cabbage in a large kettle with boiling salted water to cover. Simmer covered 5 minutes. Remove from water, drain well, and cool slightly. Carefully peel back 6 outside leaves. Carefully cut out center of cabbage from the top, making a hole about 3 inches wide and 2 inches deep. Sprinkle cavity with ¼ teaspoon salt. Chop removed cabbage to make ½ cup; set aside.

In large skillet, melt butter. Add onion and cook until tender, about 5 minutes. Remove from heat. Add celery and leaves, parsley, corned beef, potatoes, remaining ½ teaspoon salt, pepper, caraway, and reserved ½ cup chopped cabbage. Mix well and pack into cavity of cabbage. Reshape turned-back leaves to cover opening. Wrap cabbage in cheesecloth. Place on a rack in a large pot. Add 1 inch of boiling water. Steam covered over moderately low heat for 30 minutes.

Cook Until Tender-Crisp

Vegetables are iffy. There are a few general cooking rules to guide you. Root vegetables take longer to cook than those that grow above the ground. Cut-up vegetables cook in less time than whole ones, and the smaller the pieces the shorter the cooking time. "Tender" means that a two-tined fork or a small, thin knife blade meets no resistance when you stick the vegetable with it. "Tender-crisp" means that you will meet some resistance. Some vegetables—potatoes are a sterling example—should never be cooked tender-crisp, and if your family's reaction to any vegetable cooked to that state is, "Hey, this stuff isn't done!" you may as well go back to cooking everything until tender. There's no point—and no nutrition—in cooking foods nobody will eat.

How long? Potatoes and other root vegetables will be tender in roughly 20 minutes if cut into medium pieces. New potatoes take a bit longer to cook than old ones, and whole new potatoes, unless they are tiny, will be tender in about 30 to 35 minutes. Beets, unless they are very small and garden-fresh, require 40 to 50 minutes, because beets are always cooked whole to avoid "bleeding"; if they are very old, they may need an hour or more.

Celery and onions, sliced, will be tender-crisp in 8 to 10 minutes, tender in 15 to 20, depending on age. Ditto green and wax beans, and peas. Cauliflower, broken into flowerets, is tender in about 12 minutes, unless it's very old; this is another vegetable that doesn't take too kindly to the tender-crisp treatment—if you like it crisp, serve it raw. Broccoli, if you split the stems, takes about the same time or a little less. Coarsely shredded cabbage can be "panned" in butter and a very little water in 6 to 8 minutes; quartered, it will take 15 to 20. Spinach, cooked in only the water that clings to the leaves, is ready in 3 to 5 minutes (frozen spinach should be thawed before cooking, or cooked long enough to thaw it). Corn on the cob, if it's young and fresh, cooks in 5 minutes after water returns to a boil; pan corn off the cob in butter and a little cream in 3 minutes.

Pork-Stuffed Cabbage

Makes 6 servings
- 1 large cabbage
- 2 tablespoons butter or margarine
- ½ cup chopped fresh onion
- 1 clove garlic, minced
- ¼ cup chopped fresh parsley
- 1 cup chopped peeled tomato
- ½ cup soft bread crumbs
- 1 teaspoon salt, divided
- ¼ teaspoon dried leaf thyme
- ½ pound ground pork

Remove outside leaves from cabbage. Place cabbage in a large kettle with boiling salted water to cover. Simmer covered 5 minutes. Remove from water, drain well, and cool slightly. Carefully peel back 6 outside leaves. Carefully cut out center of cabbage from the top, making a hole about 3 inches wide and 2 inches deep. Sprinkle cavity with ¼ teaspoon salt. Chop removed cabbage to make ½ cup; set aside.

In large skillet, melt butter. Add onion and garlic; cook until tender, about 5 minutes. Add remaining ingredients and reserved chopped cabbage. Mix well and pack into cavity of cabbage. Reshape turned-back leaves to cover opening. Wrap cabbage in cheesecloth. Place on a rack in a large pot. Add 1 inch of boiling water. Steam covered over moderately low heat for 30 minutes.

Stuffed Cabbage, Dutch Style

Makes 6 servings
- 1 pound ground chuck
- ½ pound ground raw pork
- 1½ cups cooked rice
- 1 medium onion, chopped
- ⅛ teaspoon *each* thyme, paprika, sage, and pepper
- ¼ teaspoon ground caraway
- 12 large leaves green cabbage (do not use tough outer leaves)
- 2 cans (10¾ ounces each) Campbell's Condensed Tomato Soup

Combine chuck, pork, rice, onion, spices, and caraway. Drop 12 cabbage leaves into boiling salted water and simmer for 5 minutes. Drain and cool. Divide meat mixture among leaves and roll up so that cabbage completely encloses meat. Place rolls side by side in a single layer in a 13x9x2-inch pan. Cover with the tomato soup. Bake covered in a preheated 350°F. oven for about 1 hour, or until the cabbage is tender.

Stuffed Fresh Artichokes (page 27). Campbell Soup Company

Shrimp Gumbo in a Bread Basket (page 33). Photo courtesy of Thomas J. Lipton, Inc.

Cauliflower with Onion Sauce

Makes 6 servings
- 1 large head cauliflower
- 1 cup boiling water
- 1 tablespoon cornstarch dissolved in 2 tablespoons water
- 1 Herb-Ox Vegetarian Style Bouillon Cube or 1 teaspoon Herb-Ox Instant Vegetarian Bouillon
- Paprika

Trim stem from cauliflower and place cauliflower in saucepan. Dissolve bouillon cube or instant bouillon in boiling water; add. Cook uncovered 3 minutes. Cover the pan; cook until cauliflower is just tender, but still crisp. Remove cauliflower and keep warm. Mix cornstarch and water, add to boiling liquid in pan, cook, stirring, until sauce is thickened. Pour sauce over cauliflower and sprinkle with paprika.

Q. *What's the best way to remove corn kernels from the cob for such dishes as fritters and custards?*
A. There's a gadget for this, called a corn stripper, that works very well. Lacking that, stand the ear of corn on a plate, stem (flat) end down. For whole kernels, simply slice them off with a sharp knife. For the milky interior, without the skin, draw the point of a sharp paring knife down the center of each row of kernels; then, with the dull side of the knife, scrape them off the cob.

Special Carrots

Makes 6 servings

  5 large carrots, grated
  2 eggs
  2 tablespoons all-purpose flour
  ½ teaspoon salt
  ¼ teaspoon white pepper
  ¼ cup chopped pecans
  3 tablespoons cooking oil, divided
  2 onions, thinly sliced
  2 stalks celery, diced
  1 green pepper, seeded and in chunks
  1½ cups peeled, seeded, and chopped tomatoes
  ¼ cup tomato paste
  ¼ cup brown sugar

Combine carrots, eggs, flour, salt, pepper, and pecans. Preheat Sunbeam Multi-Cooker Frypan to 350°F. Place 2 tablespoons of the oil in Frypan. Drop mixture into Frypan by teaspoonfuls. Fry until these patties are brown on both sides. Drain on paper towels. Add remaining oil to Frypan; add remaining ingredients. Turn Frypan temperature to Simmer and cook vegetables 10 minutes, stirring occasionally. Taste and season. Carefully add patties; simmer covered 10 minutes.

Orange-Carrots in Cream

Makes 4 servings

  1 pound carrots, peeled and shredded
  2 tablespoons orange juice
  2 tablespoons butter or margarine, melted
  ½ cup half and half
  1 egg yolk
  ½ teaspoon salt
     Dash ground nutmeg
     Chopped fresh parsley

Combine carrots, orange juice, and butter in 3-cup baking dish; cover. Bake in preheated 350°F. oven for 15 minutes. Blend half and half, egg yolk, salt, and nutmeg. Stir into carrot mixture. Bake 15 minutes, or until set. Let stand 3 minutes. Garnish with parsley.

Parmesan Cauliflower

Makes 6 servings

  1 small head cauliflower
     Salt to taste
  6 tablespoons grated Parmesan cheese
  ½ cup heavy cream
  ¾ cup fresh bread crumbs
  2 tablespoons butter or margarine, melted
     Toasted sliced almonds

Trim cauliflower and place in a medium saucepan with ½ cup water. Cook covered 6 to 7 minutes until somewhat tender. Drain well. Break cauliflower into cauliflowerets and slice ½ inch thick. Layer one-third of the cauliflower in a 2-quart casserole. Sprinkle lightly with salt and 2 tablespoons cheese. Repeat layers twice. Pour cream over cauliflower. Top with bread crumbs and drizzle with butter. Preheat oven to 350°F. Bake 20 to 25 minutes, until cauliflower is tender and topping is lightly browned. Sprinkle with almonds before serving.

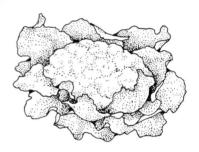

Baked Carrot-Raisin Medley

Makes 6 servings

  ¾ cup Sun-Maid® Seedless Raisins
  1 large baking apple, thinly sliced
  3 cups thinly sliced carrots
  1 lemon, divided
  ¼ cup honey
  ¾ teaspoon ground cinnamon
  ½ teaspoon salt
  2 tablespoons butter or margarine
     Chopped parsley

Preheat the oven to 400°F. Combine the raisins, apple, and carrots in a large bowl. Cut the lemon in half and add the juice from one half along with the honey, cinnamon, and salt, mixing well. Turn the mixture into a greased 2-quart heat-proof casserole. Thinly slice the remaining lemon half and arrange the slices on top. Cover and bake for 1 hour, or until the carrots are tender. Serve dotted with butter and sprinkled with parsley.

Cucumber Boats

Makes 8 servings

4 small cucumbers
2 tablespoons grated onion
¼ cup finely chopped celery
2 tablespoons snipped parsley
8 large mushrooms, chopped
4 tablespoons finely diced Swiss cheese
French Dressing (see index)
Salt and pepper to taste

Peel cucumbers and cut in half lengthwise. With a spoon, scoop out the seeds and the membrane around them, leaving small "boats." Combine onion, celery, parsley, mushrooms, and cheese with just enough French Dressing to coat the ingredients. Season to taste. Mound into cucumber shells and refrigerate until ready to serve.

Corn Pudding

Makes 6 servings

2 cups milk or half and half
¼ cup butter or margarine
4 eggs
2 cups whole-kernel corn
6 slices bacon, cooked and crumbled, or ¼ cup minced ham
2 teaspoons sugar
½ teaspoon salt
⅛ teaspoon white pepper
2 tablespoons chopped fresh parsley

Combine milk and butter in small saucepan. Heat until steaming. Beat eggs lightly in bowl. Gradually beat in hot milk mixture. Stir in corn, bacon, sugar, salt, and pepper. Pour into greased 1½-quart casserole. Place casserole in large baking pan. Add boiling water to come halfway up side of casserole. Bake at 325°F. for 1 hour, or until knife inserted in center comes out clean. Let stand 10 minutes. Sprinkle with parsley.

Shrimp Gumbo in a Bread Basket

Makes about 1 quart

1 round loaf unsliced bread (about 9 inches diameter)
¼ cup melted butter or margarine
1 envelope Lipton® Tomato-Onion Recipe Soup Mix
2 cups water
⅛ to ¼ teaspoon hot pepper sauce
1 package (8 ounces) frozen sliced okra
2 frozen ears corn, partially thawed and quartered
1 pound uncooked shrimp, cleaned

Preheat oven to 400°F. Cut lengthwise slice off top of bread. Hollow out center, leaving ½-inch shell. Brush bottom and sides of shell with butter and bake 10 minutes.

Meanwhile, in a large saucepan, combine Lipton Tomato-Onion Recipe Soup Mix, water, and hot pepper sauce; bring to a boil. Add okra and corn and cook, stirring occasionally, 15 minutes. Stir in shrimp and cook 5 minutes, or until shrimp are tender. Spoon shrimp, corn, and okra into hot bread shell; pour soup mixture into small crock or bowl. Into each serving bowl, spoon in shrimp mixture; top with tomato-onion soup mixture. Serve with bread shell, cut in wedges.

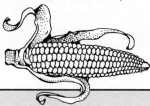

On the Cob—or Off

Everyone loves fresh corn; to prepare, remember, hurry, hurry! Strip away husks and silk (a dry vegetable brush gets obstinate silk from between rows of kernels) just before cooking. Have ready a large kettle of boiling water. Do not salt it (salt makes the corn tough); for fresh-tasting sweetness, you may add a tablespoon or so of sugar if you like. If you suspect the corn of being close to retirement age, make the cooking liquid half water, half milk. Rinse the corn briefly in cold water. Add to the pot, bring again to a boil, and boil gently no more than 5 minutes for young corn, 6 or 7 for older.

If it becomes absolutely necessary to cook corn that must be held for a time, pack the prepared ears into a pan that has a tight-fitting lid. Do not salt, but add ½ teaspoon sugar and 1 inch of water. Cover and place over the lowest possible heat for 15 minutes or longer—as long as dinner will be delayed up to ¾ hour. This method cooks corn by steaming. If you are cooking as many as a dozen ears or more, you may even extend the holding time up to an hour. The corn will not be quite as toothsome as when briefly cooked, but this way serves far better than endlessly boiling it.

To remove kernels from the cob before cooking, cut off with a sharp knife. Or, if you wish only the sweet, tender interior of the kernel, cut down the middle of each row of kernels with the tip of a sharp knife, slitting the kernels but not reaching the cob; then scrape off the milky contents with the blunt side of the knife. A stripper, a gadget that looks like giant tweezers with a central toothed circle, is available to strip kernels readily from the cob.

Baked Mushrooms (page 36). Caloric Corporation

Eggplant Lasagna

Makes 6 to 8 servings
  2 tablespoons butter or margarine
  ½ cup chopped fresh onion
  4 fresh tomatoes (4 cups), peeled and chopped
  ½ cup chopped fresh parsley, divided
  ¾ teaspoon salt, divided
  ½ teaspoon sugar
  ½ teaspoon pepper, divided
  ½ teaspoon dried leaf oregano
  1 teaspoon fresh lemon juice
  2 cups (1 pound) creamed cottage cheese
  ¼ cup grated Parmesan cheese
  1 egg
  2 eggplants
  ½ cup all-purpose flour
  ⅓ cup salad oil
  ½ pound mozzarella cheese, sliced

In large saucepan, melt butter. Add onion and cook until tender. Add tomatoes, ¼ cup parsley, ½ teaspoon salt, sugar, ⅛ teaspoon pepper, oregano, and lemon juice. Simmer uncovered for 30 minutes; remove from heat. In medium bowl, mix cottage cheese, Parmesan cheese, remaining ¼ cup chopped parsley, egg, remaining ¼ teaspoon salt, and ⅛ teaspoon pepper.

Pare eggplants, cut in ½-inch slices and dust with flour. Heat oil in large skillet, add eggplant, and brown on both sides. Remove as browned. In a shallow 2-quart baking dish, arrange a layer of eggplant, spread with half of cottage cheese mixture, spoon half of tomato sauce over cottage cheese, and top with half of mozzarella cheese. Repeat with remaining eggplant, cottage cheese, tomato sauce, and mozzarella cheese. Bake uncovered in 350°F. oven 30 minutes. Let stand 5 minutes before serving.

Eggplant Fans

Makes 4 servings
  2 cups thinly sliced onions
  4 cloves garlic, minced or pressed
  ½ cup Mazola Corn Oil
  ¼ cup lemon juice
  1 teaspoon dried basil leaves
  1 teaspoon dried oregano leaves
  1 teaspoon salt
  ⅛ teaspoon pepper
  2 small eggplants (about 1 pound each), ends trimmed
  1¾ pounds (about) ripe tomatoes, halved lengthwise, cored, and cut into thin wedges
  ¾ pound (about) small zucchini, thinly sliced

In large bowl, toss together onions, garlic, corn oil, lemon juice, basil, oregano, salt, and pepper. Place about 2 cups in bottom of 13x9x2-inch baking dish. Split eggplants lengthwise. Cut each half lengthwise into ½-inch strips, leaving slices attached at stem end to form fans. Slip tomato and zucchini slices into the slits of the eggplant halves. Arrange the eggplant halves, gently forced together, side by side, in prepared baking dish. Top with remaining onion mixture. Cover with foil. Bake in 450°F. oven 10 minutes. Reduce temperature to 350°F.; bake 1 hour longer, or until eggplants are tender. Serve hot, at room temperature, or cold.

Puffed Baked Eggplant

Makes 4 servings
  2 medium eggplants (¾ pounds each)
  ¾ cup water
  4 eggs, separated
  1 can (7 ounces) SPAM®, finely chopped
  ¾ cup soft bread crumbs
  ⅓ cup grated Parmesan cheese
  ¼ teaspoon garlic salt
  ⅛ teaspoon ground nutmeg
  ⅛ teaspoon pepper

Halve each eggplant lengthwise. Scoop out pulp leaving a ¼-inch shell. Coarsely chop pulp; cook in water in small covered saucepan 15 minutes, or until tender; drain if necessary. Mash cooked pulp; stir in egg yolks. Mix in SPAM®, bread crumbs, cheese, garlic salt, nutmeg, and pepper. Whip egg whites until stiff but not dry; fold into SPAM® mixture. Pile into eggplant shells; place in baking dish just large enough to hold them. Bake in 325°F. oven 35 to 40 minutes, or until puffed and lightly browned.

Eggplant Fans; Salsa (page 126); Marinated Tomato Salad (page 73); White Gazpacho (page 48). Mazola Corn Oil

Stuffed Eggplant

Makes 4 servings

  1 large eggplant
  ½ cup water
  ½ teaspoon salt
  ¼ cup chopped onion
  1 tablespoon butter
  1 can (10½ ounces) Campbell's Condensed
      Cream of Mushroom Soup
  1 teaspoon Worcestershire sauce
  1 cup fine butter-type cracker crumbs (about 24
      crackers)
  1 tablespoon chopped parsley
1½ cups water

Slice off one side of eggplant. Remove pulp to within
½ inch of skin. Dice removed pulp and place in saucepan. Add water and salt. Simmer until eggplant is
tender. Drain. Sauté onion in butter until golden
brown. Stir onion, mushroom soup, Worcestershire
sauce, and all but 2 tablespoons of the cracker crumbs
into eggplant pulp. Fill eggplant shell with mixture.
Place eggplant in a shallow baking pan. Sprinkle top
with reserved crumbs and parsley. Pour water into
baking pan. Bake in a preheated 375°F. oven for 1 hour
or until piping hot.

Lettuce Bundles

Makes 8 servings

  1 whole chicken breast (about 1 pound), split
  ½ cup Smucker's Low Sugar Orange Marmalade
  ½ cup cooked rice
  ¼ cup chopped green onions
  4 teaspoons soy sauce
  ⅛ teaspoon crushed red pepper
  1 large head iceberg lettuce
     Tops of large green onions (about 8 inches long)

Place chicken, skin side down, on broiler rack over a
pan. Broil about 4 inches from heat source for 20
minutes; turn and continue to broil until chicken is
fork-tender. Cool chicken; remove skin and bones. Pull
chicken meat into shreds and place in a bowl. Add
orange marmalade, rice, chopped onions, soy sauce,
and pepper. Chill.

Remove core from lettuce. Separate lettuce into individual leaves. Using tongs, dip each leaf into a large
saucepan of boiling water just until wilted. Drain well
on paper towels. Cut out the coarse, heavy stems at the
base of the lettuce leaves. Dip green onion tops into

lettuce leaf into about a 4½-inch square. (You may
need to piece some leaves together to form a square.)
Place ½ tablespoon of chicken filling diagonally across
the lettuce. Bring one corner up over filling; bring two
opposite ends toward center to enclose filling and roll
up to form an envelopelike package. Tie with a green
onion string across the center of each package. Continue stuffing lettuce leaves until the filling has been
used.

Arrange bundles on plate and refrigerate until serving time. If prepared ahead, drain off any moisture that
accumulates in plate before serving.

Croûte of Mushrooms

Makes 6 servings

  2 tablespoons butter
  2 tablespoons chopped onion
  1 pound fresh mushrooms, sliced
  1 can (10½ ounces) Campbell's Condensed
      Cream of Chicken Soup
  ¼ cup white wine
  1 tablespoon lemon juice
  6 toast slices

Melt butter and sauté onion until golden. Add mushrooms and sauté until wilted. Stir in soup, wine, and
lemon juice. Cook until bubbly, then simmer 10
minutes. Spoon hot over toast slices.

Baked Mushrooms

Makes 4 to 6 servings

  1 pound mushrooms, sliced
  1 onion, minced
  1 clove garlic, minced
  ¼ cup butter or margarine
  1 tablespoon cornstarch
  2 tablespoons dry sherry
  1 teaspoon Dijon mustard
  ½ teaspoon Worcestershire sauce
  ½ teaspoon salt
  1 cup fresh bread crumbs
  1 tablespoon grated Parmesan cheese
     Snipped fresh parsley

In large skillet, heat butter and sauté mushrooms,
onion, and garlic until tender. Combine cornstarch and
sherry in small bowl; stir until smooth. Blend in mustard, Worcestershire sauce, and salt. Transfer mushroom mixture to 1½-quart ovenproof casserole. Add
sherry-Worcestershire mixture. Sprinkle with bread
crumbs and cheese. Preheat oven to 375°F. Bake 15
minutes, or until mushroom mixture is thickened and
topping is lightly browned. Sprinkle with parsley.

Mushroom-Rice Ring Amandine

Makes 8 servings
- ¼ cup butter or margarine
- 2½ cups (½ pound) sliced mushrooms
- ¾ cup chopped onions
- 1¾ cups uncooked processed rice
- 1 can (10¾ ounces) condensed chicken broth
- 2¾ cups water
- 1 tablespoon Lea & Perrins Worcestershire Sauce
- ½ teaspoon salt
- ⅓ cup toasted sliced almonds
- ¼ cup chopped parsley
- 2 packages (10 ounces each) frozen green peas, cooked and drained

In a large skillet, melt butter. Add mushrooms and onions; sauté until tender, about 5 minutes. Stir in rice, broth, water, Lea & Perrins, and salt. Bring to boiling point. Reduce heat and simmer covered until rice is tender and liquid is absorbed, about 25 minutes. Stir in almonds and parsley. Pack into a buttered 6-cup ring mold. Unmold onto a heated platter. Fill center of ring with hot peas.

The Ubiquitous Mushroom

There's no middle course with mushrooms—you either love them or hate them. To mushroom lovers, a garnish of sautéed mushrooms, or a big, fluted mushroom cap crowning a chop or filet mignon, or a garland of them around a steak or a roast of beef is a sight to bring tears to the eyes.

Sherry-sautéed mushrooms: Wipe 1 pound of mushrooms clean with a damp cloth. Quarter the large ones through the stems; leave the small ones whole. In a skillet, combine the mushrooms, 2 tablespoons of butter, and ¼ cup of sherry; cover the mushrooms and cook them over high heat for 2 minutes. Uncover them and continue to cook them until the liquid evaporates. Continue to cook them, stirring constantly, over high heat until they are lightly browned. Season them to taste with salt and pepper.

Deviled Mushrooms

Makes 12 appetizers
- 12 medium-size mushrooms (about 1½ inches in diameter)
  - Salt
- ½ cup minced ham
- 2 tablespoons finely chopped shallots
- 1 tablespoon prepared mustard
- 2 teaspoons mayonnaise
  - Dash pepper
- 3 or 4 pimiento-stuffed green olives, sliced

Preheat oven to 375°F. Wipe mushrooms gently with damp cloth. Remove stems carefully and reserve for another purpose. Place mushroom caps, rounded side down, in 8-inch baking dish. Sprinkle very lightly with salt. Mix ham, shallots, mustard, mayonnaise, and pepper. Spoon into mushroom caps. Bake 12 minutes. Top with olive slices, arrange on platter, and serve immediately.

This recipe was provided by the makers of Saran Wrap™ brand plastic film.

Mushrooms Bordelaise

Makes 4 servings
- 1 cup red wine
- ¼ cup chopped shallots or white onions
  - Dash black pepper
  - Dash crumbled thyme
- ½ bay leaf
- 1 can (10½ ounces) Campbell's Condensed Beef Broth
- ¼ cup all-purpose flour mixed with ½ cup water
- 1 pound small button mushrooms
- ¼ cup butter
  - Buttered toast slices

In a saucepan, combine red wine, shallots, pepper, thyme, bay leaf, and beef broth. Simmer for 15 minutes. Stir in flour mixture and continue stirring over low heat until sauce bubbles and thickens. Sauté mushrooms in butter until golden brown and cooked. Remove bay leaf from sauce; fold in mushrooms. Serve over thin slices of well-buttered toast.

Golden Idaho Harvest-Stuffed Potatoes (page 41). Idaho Potato Commission

Q. *A recipe I'd like to try calls for onion juice. How on earth do you juice an onion?*
A.   As with an orange, cut it in half and ream it on a juicer. (Give the juicer a thorough bath afterward.) You can also buy onion juice in small bottles, handy where the flavor without the texture is desirable.

California Mushrooms

Makes 8 servings
  1½ **pounds mushrooms**
  ¼ **cup butter**
    Salt and white pepper to taste
  1 **cup sour cream**
  2 **tablespoons chopped fresh dill or 2 teaspoons dried dill weed**

Wash mushrooms and pat dry. Trim stems, if necessary, and cut into slices through both cap and stem. Melt butter in a large skillet and sauté mushrooms until lightly browned. (At this point you may leave them—the heat turned off, of course—until just before serving time. Heat, and continue.) Turn heat low; season mushrooms lightly with salt and pepper. Distribute sour cream over mushrooms in spoonfuls and stir in. Heat, but do not allow to boil. Garnish with dill. Serve at once.

Stuffed Onions

Makes 6 servings
  6 **medium-size onions**
  1 **cup fresh bread crumbs**
  ½ **cup chopped fresh parsley**
  1 **tomato, peeled and chopped**
  2 **tablespoons chopped pine nuts or almonds**
  1 **clove garlic, minced**
  ¼ **teaspoon salt**

Peel onions; cut off about ½ inch at stem end of each and trim root end close. Place in a saucepan, add ½ cup water, and cover. Cook 10 to 15 minutes, or until onions are somewhat tender. Let stand a few minutes to cool. Remove the center of each onion with a small spoon, leaving ¼-inch-thick walls. (Reserve centers for use at another time.) Combine remaining ingredients. Spoon into onion shells. Place in baking dish; add 2 tablespoons water. Preheat oven to 375°F. Bake 20 minutes, or until filling is slightly crusty and onions are tender.

Hash-Stuffed Peppers (page 40). Lea & Perrins

Salad-Stuffed Peppers

Makes 4 servings

4 green peppers, halved and seeded
1 can (7 ounces) SPAM®, diced
1 can (8 ounces) whole-kernel corn, drained
½ cup chopped celery
¼ cup shredded Monterey Jack cheese
1 tablespoon minced onion
Dash pepper
3 tablespoons Italian dressing
3 cups shredded lettuce
1 can pimientos, cut into strips

Simmer pepper halves in boiling water 2 minutes, making sure peppers are completely covered. Drain and rinse with cold water; refrigerate until cold. Combine SPAM®, corn, celery, cheese, onion, and pepper; mix with dressing. Spoon onto pepper halves. Divide lettuce into 4 salad plates; place 2 filled peppers on each plate. Garnish tops with pimiento strips.

Confetti Hash Peppers

Makes 3 servings

3 medium green peppers (about ¾ pound)
1 can (15 ounces) Mary Kitchen Roast Beef Hash
½ cup frozen whole-kernel corn, thawed
¼ cup chopped onion
2 tablespoons chili sauce
⅓ cup shredded cheddar cheese

Cut off tops of peppers; remove seeds. Cook in boiling water to cover 3 minutes; drain. Combine hash, corn, onion, and chili sauce; pile into pepper halves. Place peppers in lightly greased baking dish. Bake in 375°F. oven 20 minutes. Sprinkle with cheese; bake 10 minutes longer.

Hash-Stuffed Peppers

Makes 6 servings

6 medium-size green peppers
1 cup water
½ teaspoon salt
2 tablespoons butter or margarine
½ cup minced onion
2 cups diced cooked corned beef
1 cup diced cooked potatoes
½ cup soft bread crumbs
1 can (8 ounces) tomato sauce
1 tablespoon Lea & Perrins Worcestershire Sauce

Cut a thin slice from the stem of each green pepper; scoop out seeds. In a large saucepan, bring water and salt to boiling point. Add peppers. Simmer covered for 5 minutes; remove peppers and drain. In a medium saucepan, melt butter. Add onion; sauté for 2 minutes. Stir in remaining ingredients. Spoon into pepper shells. Place in a greased 10x6x1½-inch baking pan. Bake uncovered in a preheated moderate oven (350°F.) until hot, about 30 minutes.

Stuffed Pepper Appetizers

Makes 12 servings

⅔ cup finely chopped onions
2 cloves garlic, minced
2 tablespoons olive oil
3 cups chicken broth
1¼ cups Uncle Ben's® Converted® Brand Rice
2 teaspoons seasoned salt
⅛ teaspoon powdered saffron
6 medium green peppers
Water
Paprika
Anchovy fillets

Cook onions and garlic in olive oil until browned. Add chicken broth and bring to boil. Stir in rice and seasoned salt. Cover tightly and cook over low heat 15 minutes. Stir in saffron and continue cooking until water is absorbed—about 10 minutes more. Cut stems out of green peppers; remove seeds. Cut thin slice off bottoms to level. Stuff rice mixture firmly into peppers. Put in heavy casserole or Dutch oven with cover. Add water to ½-inch depth. Cover and bring to a simmer over medium heat. Cook 10 to 15 minutes, or until peppers are soft but still crisp. Chill. Cut in half lengthwise and garnish each half with a sprinkling of paprika and an anchovy fillet.

The Pep in Peppers

The most familiar peppers in this country's cuisine are the big, handsome green, red, and yellow sweet peppers that we use for such dishes as pepper steak and stuffed peppers, as well as in many sauces and salads. But since we're becoming more and more appreciative of Mexican cooking, we're learning to use chilies, too—the smaller hot peppers that are a vital part of south-of-the-border cooking. All are hot, but they range from a mild burn to a conflagration, so choose wisely. Always wear rubber gloves when you're cutting up chilies, and keep your hands away from your eyes. Be sure to remove all the seeds—they are hotter than the flesh of the peppers, and are often bitter as well.

Company Potato Pie

Makes 4 servings

1½ pounds potatoes, pared and cut in chunks
⅔ cup milk, divided
2 eggs, divided
1¼ cups shredded sharp cheddar cheese, divided
¼ teaspoon pepper, divided
1 pound ground beef
1 medium carrot, shredded (½ cup)
1 medium onion, chopped (½ cup)
2 small cloves garlic, minced
¼ cup packaged dry bread crumbs
2 tablespoons Dijon-style mustard

Steam potatoes in 1-inch boiling salted water 20 to 25 minutes, until tender. Drain. Mash potatoes in large bowl. Beat in ⅓ cup milk, 1 egg, ½ cup shredded cheese, and ⅛ teaspoon pepper. Reserve 1 cup mashed potatoes for garnish; spread remaining potatoes on bottom and sides of 9-inch pie plate (but not over rim). Bake in 400°F. oven 10 minutes. In medium bowl, combine beef, carrot, onion, garlic, bread crumbs, mustard, remaining ¾ cup cheese, ⅓ cup milk, 1 egg, and ⅛ teaspoon pepper; mix well. Spoon meat mixture into partially baked potato shell. Using a pastry bag fitted with a decorators' tip, pipe reserved mashed potatoes around edge of pie plate and across top in crisscross fashion. Bake in 350°F. oven 35 minutes. Let sit 5 minutes before serving. Cut into wedges.

Golden Idaho Harvest-Stuffed Potatoes

Makes 4 servings

4 Idaho® Potatoes
1 egg
¼ cup milk
2 tablespoons butter or margarine
¼ cup finely chopped red or green pepper
2 tablespoons finely chopped onion
1 cup (4 ounces) shredded cheddar cheese
1 teaspoon salt
¼ teaspoon pepper
¼ teaspoon dried leaf basil

Scrub potatoes, dry, and prick with a fork. Bake in 425°F. oven 55 to 65 minutes, until soft. Reduce oven to 350°F. When potatoes are done, cut a slice from top of each. Carefully scoop out potato without breaking skin. Set skins aside. Place potato in medium mixing bowl. Beat in egg, milk, and butter; beat until smooth. Stir in remaining ingredients. Spoon potato mixture into reserved potato skins. Bake in a 350°F. oven 25 to 30 minutes, or until heated through.

Spinach Soufflé Crêpes

Makes 8 servings

2 eggs
½ cup all-purpose flour
¼ teaspoon salt
¾ cup milk
Butter or margarine, divided
1 can (12 ounces) SPAM®
1 package (12 ounces) frozen spinach soufflé, slightly thawed
Cheese Sauce (recipe follows)

In small bowl, beat eggs. Add flour and salt; mix until smooth. Slowly add milk. Melt 1 tablespoon butter; stir into batter. Cover and refrigerate at least 1 hour.

To make crêpes, heat 8-inch omelet pan until hot; add ½ teaspoon butter. Pour a scant ¼ cup batter; tilt and turn pan to spread batter evenly over bottom. Bake until lightly browned on bottom; turn to brown other side. Repeat to make 8 crêpes.

Cut SPAM® into 8 long pieces; cut each piece in half lengthwise. To assemble crêpes, place 2 strips SPAM® on each crêpe; top with ¼ cup spinach soufflé; roll up loosely. Place in lightly greased baking dish, seam side down. Repeat with remaining crêpes. Bake in 400°F. oven 20 minutes. Pour Cheese Sauce over top; bake 5 minutes longer.

Nice to know: Crêpes can be prepared the night before, stacked between sheets of waxed paper, and refrigerated until you're ready to fill them.

Cheese Sauce

1 tablespoon butter or margarine
1 tablespoon all-purpose flour
⅛ teaspoon salt
⅛ teaspoon dry mustard
Pepper to taste
¾ cup milk
¼ teaspoon Worcestershire sauce
½ cup (2 ounces) grated sharp cheddar cheese

In small saucepan, melt butter; blend in flour, salt, mustard, and pepper. Add milk and Worcestershire; stir until smooth. Cook and stir over medium heat until mixture thickens and boils. Add cheese; stir over low heat just until cheese melts.

Holiday Green Bean Casserole (page 28). Durkee Famous Foods

Acorn Squash High-Rise

Makes 8 servings

  2 **large acorn squash, about 2 pounds each**
  ¼ **cup butter or margarine**
  2 **tablespoons brown sugar**
  ½ **teaspoon salt**
  ¼ **teaspoon freshly grated orange peel**
  ⅛ **teaspoon ground nutmeg**
      Dash pepper
  4 **eggs, separated**
  ¼ **cup chopped pecans**

Cut each squash in half. Scoop out seeds. In large covered saucepan, steam squash in 2 inches boiling water 30 to 35 minutes, or until tender. Drain and scrape pulp (about 3 cups) from squash shells. In large bowl of electric mixer, blend squash on low speed until smooth. Add butter, brown sugar, salt, orange peel, nutmeg, and pepper. Blend until smooth. Add egg yolks; beat until light. In small bowl of electric mixer, beat egg whites on high speed until stiff. Fold into squash mixture. Pour into a 1½-quart soufflé or baking dish. Sprinkle with pecans. Bake in a 350°F. oven 55 to 60 minutes, or until set.

Savory Scalloped Tomatoes

Makes 8 servings

  3 **tablespoons butter or margarine, divided**
  1 **cup diced celery**
 ½ **cup chopped onion**
  2 **tablespoons all-purpose flour**
  1 **can (1 pound 12 ounces) tomatoes**
  4 **teaspoons Lea & Perrins Worcestershire Sauce**
  1 **tablespoon sugar**
  1 **teaspoon salt**
  4 **slices toasted white bread, divided**

In a medium saucepan, melt 2 tablespoons of the butter. Add celery and onion; cook until tender, about 5 minutes. Blend in flour; cook and stir 1 minute. Remove from heat. Stir in tomatoes (do not crush), Lea & Perrins, sugar, and salt. Spread toast with remaining 1 tablespoon butter; cut into ½-inch cubes. Stir half of the bread cubes into the tomato mixture. Turn into a buttered 1½-quart casserole. Bake uncovered in a preheated moderate oven (350°F.) for 30 minutes. Top with reserved bread cubes; bake 10 to 12 minutes longer.

Savory Scalloped Tomatoes. Lea & Perrins

Easy Stuffed Tomatoes

Makes 6 servings
  6 slices bread
  6 firm tomatoes
  1 small onion
  6 sprigs parsley
  2 egg yolks
  ½ teaspoon salt
  ¼ teaspoon pepper
  2 tablespoons butter

Butter a baking dish. Blender-crumb bread. Wash and dry tomatoes, cut off tops, and remove pulp. Sprinkle insides of shells with salt and pepper. Put tomato pulp, onion, parsley, egg yolks, and seasonings into blender; cover and process at Chop until parsley and onion are finely chopped. Mix with bread crumbs. Melt butter in saucepan, add tomato mixture, and cook over low heat about 10 minutes. Fill tomatoes with this mixture. Sprinkle bread crumbs on top, if desired. Bake 20 to 25 minutes in a preheated 350°F. oven until soft.

Fried Tomatoes

Makes about 4 servings
  ⅓ cup fine dry bread crumbs
  ½ teaspoon sugar
  ¼ teaspoon salt
  ⅛ teaspoon pepper
  ¼ cup Mazola Corn Oil
  1 pound (about 3 medium) slightly ripe (green) or very firm ripe tomatoes, sliced about ½-inch thick

In small shallow dish, stir together bread crumbs, sugar, salt, and pepper. In large skillet, heat corn oil over medium-high heat. Coat tomato slices with crumb mixture, patting off excess. Fry, a few slices at a time, about 3 to 4 minutes, turning once, or until lightly browned. Drain on paper towels.

Swiss-Broiled Tomatoes

Makes 2 servings
  2 small ripe tomatoes
    Salt and white pepper to taste
  2 tablespoons fine dry bread crumbs
  ½ teaspoon basil
  2 teaspoons melted butter
  ¼ cup grated Swiss cheese

Cut tomatoes in half. Season lightly with salt and pepper. Mix remaining ingredients and pile lightly on tomato halves. Broil until cheese begins to melt and topping is lightly browned.

Rosemary Turnip Puff

Makes 4 to 6 servings
  1 pound turnips, peeled and cut into chunks
  ¼ cup butter or margarine, divided
  ¼ cup heavy cream or half and half
  1 egg, lightly beaten
  ½ teaspoon rosemary
  ¼ teaspoon salt
  ¾ cup fresh bread crumbs

Place turnips in 1-quart saucepan with ¾ cup water. Cook covered until tender, about 10 minutes; drain. Process in food processor or mash with potato masher. Place in casserole. Stir in 2 tablespoons butter until melted. Add cream, egg, rosemary, and salt; stir until mixed. Melt remaining 2 tablespoons butter in small skillet over medium heat. Stir in bread crumbs and sprinkle over turnip mixture. Preheat oven to 325°F. Bake 30 to 35 minutes until turnip mixture is set and topping is lightly browned.

Turnips au Gratin

Makes 6 servings
  4 cups (1½ pounds) pared, cubed fresh turnips
  1 teaspoon sugar
  1½ teaspoons salt, divided
  4 tablespoons butter or margarine, divided
  2 tablespoons all-purpose flour
  ⅛ teaspoon ground white pepper
  1½ cups milk
  ¾ cup grated sharp cheddar cheese
  ½ cup packaged dry bread crumbs

In medium saucepan, bring 1 inch water to a boil. Add turnips, sugar, and ½ teaspoon salt. Cook covered 12 minutes or until tender; drain. Remove turnips and set aside. In same saucepan, melt 2 tablespoons butter; blend in flour, remaining 1 teaspoon salt, and pepper. Cook 1 minute. Remove from heat and gradually stir in milk. Return to heat and cook, stirring constantly, until mixture boils and thickens. Add cheese, stirring until melted. In 10x6x½-inch baking dish, alternate layers of turnips and cheese sauce. In small saucepan melt remaining 2 tablespoons butter. Stir in bread crumbs. Sprinkle crumbs over turnips. Bake in a 350°F. oven 15 minutes or until crumbs are golden.

Yam Croquettes with Pineapple Sauce

Makes 3 servings

 1 can (16 ounces) cut yams
 1 can (7 ounces) SPAM®, finely chopped
 1 egg yolk
   Pepper to taste
 ½ cup bread crumbs
 1 egg, lightly beaten
   Shortening
   Pineapple Sauce (recipe follows)

Drain yams and mash. Combine with SPAM®, egg yolk, and pepper. Shape mixture into 6 balls. Roll in bread crumbs; dip in beaten egg. Roll in bread crumbs again. Refrigerate at least 1 hour for easy frying. Heat 3 inches shortening to 350°F.; slip in croquettes. Cook 3 to 4 minutes, until browned. Drain on paper towels. Serve with Pineapple Sauce.

Pineapple Sauce

 ¼ cup water
 1 teaspoon cornstarch
 1 can (8 ounces) crushed pineapple in syrup
 2 tablespoons dark brown sugar
 2 whole cloves

In small saucepan, stir together water and cornstarch until smooth. Add pineapple, sugar, and cloves. Cook and stir over medium heat until mixture thickens and boils. Simmer 2 minutes; remove cloves before serving.

Quick/Easy Creamed Vegetables

Easier than making white sauce, far superior in flavor, this way with vegetables pleases children and adults alike. Try with cut green beans, carrots, broccoli, peas, cauliflower, brussels sprouts (halved), celery—in fact, any vegetable your family likes. Try it, too, with vegetables your family doesn't like—you may make some converts. Cook vegetables as usual; drain, reserving cooking liquid. Place vegetables in serving dish and keep warm. Return ½ cup cooking liquid to pan; bring to a simmer. Cut 1 package (3 ounces) cream cheese into 6 pieces. Add to liquid 1 piece at a time, stirring until melted before adding the next piece. Season to taste. Pour over vegetables; toss lightly to combine. Serve at once. For a larger amount of vegetables, use 1 cup liquid and 1 package (8 ounces) cream cheese.

Stuffed Zucchini Boats

Makes 4 to 8 servings

 4 medium-size zucchini (1½ to 2 pounds)
 ½ cup minced onion
 1 large clove garlic, minced
 1½ tablespoons vegetable oil
 ⅓ cup Sun-Maid® Seedless Raisins
 1 teaspoon basil, crumbled
 1 teaspoon salt
 2 cups fresh bread crumbs
 ½ cup grated Parmesan cheese
   Shredded cheddar cheese

Cut the zucchini in half lengthwise and scoop out the center with the tip of a spoon, leaving a ¼-inch shell; chop the zucchini pulp. Sauté the onion and garlic in oil until the onion is soft but not browned. Add the chopped zucchini and the raisins, basil, and salt. Simmer, stirring occasionally, for a few minutes, or until the excess moisture evaporates. Preheat the oven to 375°F. Remove the zucchini mixture from heat and stir in the bread crumbs and Parmesan cheese. Spoon into the zucchini shells and place the stuffed boats in a 13x9x2-inch baking dish. Sprinkle the boats with cheddar cheese and pour ⅓ cup water into the dish. Bake covered 20 minutes; uncover and bake 5 minutes longer.

Baked Zucchini Boats

Makes 6 servings

 6 plump zucchini (about 2½ pounds)
 1 large onion, chopped
 2 tablespoons butter or margarine
 2 tablespoons long-grained rice
 ¼ teaspoon salt
 ⅛ teaspoon pepper
 ⅓ cup grated cheddar cheese
 ¼ cup chopped parsley
 1 can (12 ounces) SPAM®, cubed

Halve zucchini lengthwise; scoop out centers leaving a ¼-inch shell. Chop pulp. In medium skillet, sauté onion and chopped zucchini in butter 3 minutes. Sprinkle rice, salt, and pepper over top; mix well. Cover tightly and simmer 10 minutes, stirring once or twice. Mix in cheese and parsley. Spoon mixture into scooped-out shells. Place in lightly greased baking dish just large enough to hold squash. Set SPAM® into stuffing. Cover pan with foil. Bake in 350°F. oven 45 minutes, or until squash is tender.

Soups of the Evening

*Or of any other time of day! Light, serve-chilled summer
soups based on vegetables, and hearty, rib-sticking winter
soups that can be a meal in themselves.*

Vegetable Chowder

Makes about 3½ quarts

- ¼ cup **Mazola Margarine**
- 1 cup chopped celery
- 1 cup chopped onion
- 1 clove garlic, minced or pressed
- 4 cups beef bouillon or broth
- 3 cups peeled cubed potatoes
- 1 can (17 ounces) whole-kernel corn, undrained
- 1 can (16 ounces) whole tomatoes, undrained, coarsely chopped
- 2 cups sliced carrots
- ½ teaspoon celery seed
- ½ teaspoon ground thyme
- ½ teaspoon salt
- 2 tablespoons **Argo or Kingsford's Corn Starch**
- ¼ cup water

In 5-quart Dutch oven or saucepot, melt margarine over medium heat. Add celery, onion, and garlic. Stirring frequently, cook 3 to 4 minutes, or until tender. Add bouillon, potatoes, corn, tomatoes, carrots, celery seed, thyme, and salt. Bring to boil over medium heat. Reduce heat; cover and simmer 30 minutes, or until vegetables are tender. In small bowl, stir together cornstarch and water until smooth. Stir into soup. Stirring constantly, bring to boil over medium heat and boil 1 minute.

Hearty Vegetable Soup

Makes about 6 servings

- 2 envelopes **Lipton® Country Vegetable Recipe Soup Mix**
- 6 cups water
- 1 can (8½ ounces) lima beans, drained
- 1 cup finely shredded cabbage
- 6 slices bacon, crisp-cooked and crumbled
- ¼ teaspoon oregano

In medium saucepan, combine Lipton Country Vegetable Recipe Soup Mix, water, lima beans, cabbage, bacon, and oregano. Bring to a boil, then simmer, stirring occasionally, 10 minutes.

Minestrone Soup

Makes 3½ quarts

- 1 can (12 ounces) **SPAM®**, finely chopped
- 1 medium onion, finely chopped
- 1 rib celery, finely chopped
- 1 medium carrot, finely chopped
- 2 cloves garlic, minced
- 2 tablespoons cooking oil
- 2 quarts water
- ½ teaspoon basil
- 1 bay leaf
- 3 cups (¾ pound) chopped cabbage
- 2 medium potatoes, peeled and diced
- 2 medium tomatoes, peeled and chopped
- 1 medium zucchini, diced
- 1 small white turnip, diced
- ½ teaspoon salt
- 1 can (16 ounces) pinto beans, undrained
- ¼ cup long-grain rice
  Parmesan cheese(optional)

In large pot, sauté SPAM®, onion, celery, carrot, and garlic in oil until lightly browned, stirring often. Add water, basil, and bay leaf; bring to a boil. Simmer covered 10 minutes. Add cabbage, potatoes, tomatoes, zucchini, turnip, and salt. Cover and gently boil 15 minutes. Add pinto beans and rice; cook covered 15 minutes longer. Serve in large soup bowls with a sprinkling of grated Parmesan cheese, if desired.

Vegetable Chowder. Argo/Kingsford's Corn Starch

White Gazpacho

Makes 4 cups

   1 pound ripe tomatoes (about 3 medium)
  ¼ cup Mazola Corn Oil
  ¼ pound zucchini, thinly sliced (1 cup)
   1 cup thinly sliced green onion
   1 clove garlic, minced or pressed
   1 green and/or sweet red pepper, cut in very thin
      1-inch long strips (1 cup)
   2 tablespoons chopped parsley
   1 teaspoon salt
  ⅛ teaspoon pepper
   1 can (13¼ ounces) chicken broth (1¾ cups)
  ⅓ cup dry white wine

Peel, seed, and coarsely chop tomatoes (about 1¼ cups); drain and reserve all liquid (about ½ cup). In large skillet, heat corn oil over medium heat. Add zucchini, onions, and garlic. Stirring constantly, cook 1 minute. Stir in tomatoes, green and/or red pepper, parsley, salt, and pepper. Stirring frequently, cook 1 minute. Remove from heat. Turn into large bowl. Stir in chicken broth, reserved tomato liquid, and wine until well mixed. Cover; refrigerate several hours or overnight.

Gazpacho

Makes 6 servings

   1 can (18 ounces) tomato juice
   1 clove garlic, halved
   1 small onion, cut up
  ½ green pepper, seeded and cut up
   1 small cucumber, pared and cut up
   2 ripe tomatoes, peeled, cored, and cut up
   3 tablespoons olive oil
   3 tablespoons red wine vinegar
 1½ teaspoons salt
  ¼ teaspoon pepper
    Croutons
    Chopped onion, green pepper, tomato, and
      cucumber (optional)

Put all ingredients except croutons and chopped-vegetable garnish into blender container in order listed. Cover; blend at medium speed until vegetables are finely chopped. Chill several hours or overnight. Top with croutons. Garnish with onion, green pepper, tomatoes, and cucumber, if desired.

Farmer's Vegetable Chowder

Makes 6 servings

  ⅓ cup Land O Lakes Sweet Cream Butter
  ½ cup (1 medium) chopped onion
  ½ cup all-purpose flour
 3¼ cups water
   1 cup Flash Nonfat Dry Milk
   1 teaspoon *each* salt, basil leaves, and oregano
      leaves
  ⅛ teaspoon pepper
   1 bag (16 ounces) frozen mixed vegetables,
      thawed and drained
   6 sliced (¼-inch) wieners
   1 cup shredded Land O Lakes Pasteurized Process
      American Cheese

In heavy 4-quart saucepan, combine butter and onion. Cook over medium heat, stirring occasionally, until onion is tender, 3 to 4 minutes. Add flour, stirring constantly, until mixture is bubbly, 1 to 2 minutes. Add remaining ingredients except vegetables, wieners, and cheese. Continue cooking, stirring occasionally, until mixture comes to a full boil, 6 to 8 minutes. Continue boiling 1 minute. Add vegetables and wieners. Cook over low heat, stirring occasionally, until vegetables are tender, 10 to 15 minutes. Add cheese; stir until melted, 1 to 2 minutes.

Make-a-Meal Soup

Makes 6 to 8 servings

   1 pound ground turkey
   1 onion, chopped
   1 tablespoon pure vegetable oil
   3 cups water
   2 chicken bouillon cubes
   1 teaspoon salt
  ¼ teaspoon pepper
   1 bay leaf
  ½ teaspoon powdered thyme
   3 *each* carrots and celery ribs, sliced
  ¼ head cabbage, cut into 1-inch chunks
   3 tablespoons uncooked rice
   1 can (8 ounces) Hunt's Tomato Sauce
   1 can (15 ounces) red beans, undrained
   1 can (28 ounces) whole tomatoes

Cook ground turkey and onion in oil in Dutch oven or large kettle until onion is tender. Add remaining ingredients. Simmer covered 30 minutes.

Hearty Sausage and Vegetable Soup Bowl

Makes 4 to 6 servings

- 1 tablespoon salad oil
- 1 pound kielbasa sausage, sliced
- ½ cup chopped onion
- 1 garlic colve, crushed
- 2 cans (19 ounces each) full-strength minestrone soup
- 1 tablespoon cider vinegar
- 1 teaspoon caraway seed
- Dash ground black pepper
- ½ cup rinsed, drained sauerkraut (optional)
- ¼ cup sour cream

In a large saucepan, heat oil until hot. Add half of the kielbasa at a time; cook until lightly browned, about 1 minute on each side. Remove with a slotted spoon. Drain off all but 1 tablespoon drippings from the pan; heat until hot. Add onion and garlic; sauté until transparent, about 5 minutes. Add soup, vinegar, caraway, and black pepper. Bring to a boil. Reduce heat and simmer covered for 10 minutes. If desired, add sauerkraut during last 1 minute of cooking. Remove from heat. Top with sour cream.

Pisto Manchego

Makes 6 servings

- 1 can (10½ ounces) Campbell's Condensed French Onion Soup
- 2 leeks, chopped
- 4 canned red pimientos, cut into strips
- 3 green peppers, seeded and diced
- 2 yellow squash, cubed
- 2 large fresh tomatoes, chopped
- 2 slices boiled or smoked ham, 4x6 inches, cubed
- 2 tablespoons butter
- 2 tablespoons oil
- 4 eggs, well beaten

Combine soup, leeks, pimientos, peppers, squash, tomatoes, ham, butter, and oil. Bring to a boil, lower heat, and simmer for 30 to 35 minutes, or until mixture is thick and liquid is almost absorbed. Stir in beaten eggs, cook 2 to 3 minutes longer. (Should be consistency of thick stew.) Season to taste. Serve very hot.

Beef Vegetable Soup

Makes 8 servings

- 2 pounds beef chuck, with★ or without bone
- 6 cups water
- 1 can (28 ounces) whole tomatoes
- 2 medium onions, chopped
- 1 cup sliced celery
- 2 garlic cloves, minced
- 1 tablespoon salt
- 1¾ teaspoons chili powder
- ¼ teaspoon ground black pepper
- 1 can (20 ounces) chick-peas or red kidney beans
- Premium® Saltine Crackers

Cut beef into 1-inch cubes; place in a Dutch oven or large saucepan with next 8 ingredients. Simmer covered 2 hours, or until meat is tender, breaking up tomatoes with a spoon. Add chick-peas or kidney beans and heat about 5 minutes. Serve with Premium Saltine Crackers.

★Add bone to soup while cooking.

Stocking Up in the Kitchen

The French chef's stockpot, simmering on the back of the stove, is his key to excellent sauces, gravies, and soups. It can be yours, too, if you're very selective indeed about what you throw away. "It's not garbage, it's stock!" may not be a very elegant slogan, but it's a practical one. Keep in your freezer two large containers, one for beef, one for poultry. If your household consumes a lot of fish, make a stock-saver for that, too. Save and freeze meat bones and scraps, poultry racks and backs and wing tips, fish heads, large bones, and shells of shrimp and lobster, each in its separate container. And don't forget vegetables. Leftovers, unless they are thickly sauced, should be saved. So should cuttings and trimmings (washed in advance, of course). Some ideas: mushroom stems or bottoms of stems, celery leaves, parsley, watercress, the peeled-away—and too often thrown-away—skins of white potatoes, carrots, white turnips, onions. Cut-off ends of celery stalks. Bits and skins of tomato. Outside lettuce leaves. (True, the last two don't freeze, in the sense that they can be eaten raw after freezing, but they're fine for stock.) Anything and everything, with two exceptions: vegetables with very strong flavor, such as some rutabagas and the ribs and core of cabbage, and "bleeding" vegetables, such as beets and radishes, that lose color and stain their surroundings as they cook.

Asparagus Soup

Makes 4 servings

2 cans (10½ ounces each) Campbell's Condensed
    Cream of Asparagus Soup
2 cups light cream
1 package (10 ounces) frozen asparagus spears,
    thawed, or 2 cups fresh asparagus tips, cooked
  Salt, pepper, and sugar

Combine all ingredients in a blender and whirl until smooth. Pour into a saucepan and heat just until bubbly. Season to taste with salt, pepper, and a few grains of sugar.

Old-Time Lentil Soup

Makes 2½ quarts

1 pound lentils
2 large ribs celery with tops, cut in thirds
¼ teaspoon basil
¼ teaspoon thyme
1 medium onion, coarsely chopped
1 teaspoon garlic, minced
1 teaspoon salt
⅛ teaspoon pepper
2 quarts water
1 can (7 ounces) SPAM®, cubed
1 tablespoon white vinegar

In large pot, combine lentils, celery, carrot, onion, garlic, salt, pepper, and water; bring to a boil. Simmer covered 45 minutes. Remove from heat; cool slightly. Place half of lentils and all celery and carrot in food processor or blender; process until puréed. Return to pot. Add SPAM® to soup. Bring to a boil; simmer covered 15 minutes. Stir in vinegar. Mix well before ladling into soup bowls.

Q.   *I made my mother-in-law's lentil soup, and it was done almost three hours before the recipe said it would be. Was there something wrong with the lentils, or was it me?*
A.   It was the lentils, not you. But there was nothing wrong with them, either. You probably soaked them, as an old-fashioned recipe would direct. Today's lentils—and this is true of dried peas and beans as well—generally do not need soaking. Read the label on the box or bag and be guided by it.

Dry Beans for Hearty Meals
Dishes made with dry beans—soups, stews, chili, casseroles—are delicious, stick-to-the-ribs satisfying, economical, and, surprisingly, rich in protein. However, it is not the high-quality, complete protein found in meat, poultry, fish, and eggs, as it lacks certain of the body-builder amino acids. These can be supplied by including a dairy product in the meal with the bean dish. A glass of milk or a couple of slices of cheese will do the trick. It's useful to know that a 1-pound package (16 ounces) of dry beans yields about 2 cups; those same 2 cups when cooked will measure about 5 cups. To avoid the overnight soaking that many kinds of beans require, try this: Place the beans in a kettle, add cold water to cover. Bring to a boil over medium heat and boil two minutes. Drain, and then repeat the process. Drain again, and the beans are ready to use.

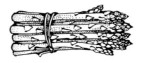

Baby Lima Chowder

Makes 6 to 8 servings

3⅓ cups drained cooked or canned white baby limas
    (reserve liquid)
  2 ounces salt pork
  ½ cup chopped onion
  2 tablespoons butter or margarine
  2 tablespoons flour
  2 cans (6½ ounces each) minced clams
1½ cups each of milk and half and half
  ½ teaspoon Worcestershire sauce
    Cayenne pepper and salt
  ½ cup sliced green onion
    Oyster crackers

Purée the cooked beans with their cooking liquid, adding enough water to make 1 to 1½ cups. Cut salt port into ½-inch cubes and fry until lightly browned. Remove salt pork and sauté chopped onion in the fat. Don't brown. Add butter; blend in flour. Drain clams; save the broth and add water to make one cup. Stir clams, broth, milk, half and half, Worcestershire sauce, and a dash of Cayenne into onion mixture. Cook and stir until thickened. Add puréed beans and salt pork. Heat thoroughly but do not boil. Salt to taste and garnish with green onion. Serve in individual bowls with oyster crackers.

Gazpacho (page 48). Hamilton Beach Scovill Inc.

Hot Borscht

Makes 12 servings

1½ pounds fresh brisket of beef, cut into ½-inch
       pieces
 1 pound beef marrow soup bones
 2 quarts water
 1 tablespoon salt
 1 can (1 pound) slivered beets
 1 can (1 pound) tomatoes, broken up
 3 tablespoons Lea & Perrins Worcestershire Sauce,
       divided
 3 cups shredded cabbage
 1 cup shredded carrots
 1 cup chopped onions
 5 sprigs parsley
 2 bay leaves
 1 teaspoon sugar
   Sour cream
   Dill (optional)

In a large saucepot, combine beef, bones, water, and
salt. Bring to boiling point. Skim off foam. Reduce
heat and simmer covered for 1½ hours. Strain beets
from liquid; set aside. Into beef broth, stir beef liquids,
tomatoes, and 2 tablespoons of the Lea & Perrins. Add
cabbage, carrots, onions, parsley, bay leaves, and sugar.
Bring to boiling point. Reduce heat and simmer covered about 20 to 30 minutes longer. Stir in reserved

Buttermilk and Beet Soup

Makes 6 servings

 1 small onion, chopped
 2 tablespoons butter or margarine
 1 cup shrimp, thawed if frozen, shelled and
       deveined
 3 cups buttermilk
 1 can (8 ounces) julienne beets, drained
½ cup Sun-Maid® Zante Currants
 1 tablespoon fresh dill, chopped, or 1 teaspoon
       dried dill weed
¼ teaspoon salt
   Dill sprigs

Sauté the onion in butter until soft but not browned.
Coarsely chop the shrimp, add to the onion in the pan,
and sauté, stirring, until they turn pink; cool. Combine
the shrimp mixture in a large bowl with the buttermilk, beets, currants, dill, and salt. Cover and refrigerate until well chilled. Serve in soup bowls, garnished
with dill sprigs.

Beet Vegetable Boredom

There are two things to remember about cooking
beets; don't peel them, and give them time. Beets that
are peeled bleed their rich, deep red into the cooking
water, and the vegetable turns out an unappetizing
brownish color. In preparing beets for cooking, wash
them carefully so that you don't break the skin, and
leave about 2 inches of both root and stem in place.
Obviously, they should be cooked whole, not sliced
or diced before they go into the pot. Young beets, half-
covered with water, will cook in 25 to 30 minutes; old
beets may take an hour and a half, or even longer.
When they are tender, let them cool a few moments.
The skins will then slip off as easily as if they were
zippered.

Young beets, with or without their greens, are delicious simply served with butter, salt, and pepper. (To
tell their age, look at their size—the smaller, the youn-
ger. Also, young beets are bright and fresh looking,
old ones darker in color.) But that is not by any means
the end of the matter.

If the beets you buy come with greens attached, save
them to use raw in salads if they are very young, or
cook whole or— if very old—cut into slivers, with the
beets or as a separate vegetable another day. Hot sliced
beets can be prepared with a sweet/sour sauce (Har-
vard beets). Or sauce them with sour cream, sprinkle
with freshly ground pepper or with grated orange peel
or with chopped dill. Or thicken the cooking water
slightly with cornstarch, season with salt, white pepper, and ample lemon juice and/or horseradish. Or
make the sauce of half cooking water, half orange juice.
Heat drained whole baby beets in a little butter, sprinkle with sugar—white or brown—and continue to
cook until they are glazed.

Beets and the richly red liquid in which they are
cooked are the chief ingredient of borscht of several
kinds, made with or without meat, served hot or cold
with a boiled potato or a dollop of sour cream.
Cooked separately so that they will not stain the whole
dish red, beets are an integral part of a proper New
England boiled dinner. Later, they are chopped and
combined with the leftover potatoes and corned beef
from that dish to make red flannel hash. Cooked beets
with apples and onions make a delicious casserole to
serve with pork.

Cold pickled beets—always with onions, vinegar,
and sugar, sometimes with oil and cloves or allspice—
are delicious summer fare. Dress up pickled beets with
sour cream for a salad. Sliced beets alternating with
thin slices of orange and, sometimes, onion, make a
refreshing salad, too. And don't forget the beet juice,
seasoned, that is the medium for pickling red beet
eggs, perfect on a picnic or with any outdoor summer
meal.

Broccoli Cream Soup

Makes about 6 cups

   2 cups chopped celery
   1 cup chopped onion
   1 package (10 ounces) frozen chopped broccoli
   1 can (10¾ ounces) condensed chicken broth
   1 cup cottage cheese
   2 cups milk
   ⅛ teaspoon pepper

Combine celery, onion, frozen broccoli, and chicken broth; bring to a boil. Cover; reduce heat and simmer 10 minutes, or until vegetables are tender. Place half of the soup mixture and cottage cheese in blender container; cover. Blend until smooth. Pour into a 3-quart saucepan. Repeat with remaining half of soup and cottage cheese. Add milk and pepper. Heat through, but do not boil. Serve immediately.

Dutch Carrot Soup

Makes 6 servings

   4 medium carrots, pared and cut up
   2 stalks celery, cut up
   1 small onion, cut up
   ¼ cup butter or margarine
   2 cans (14 ounces each) beef broth
   3 tablespoons farina
   1 teaspoon salt
   ⅛ teaspoon pepper
   ⅛ teaspoon ground nutmeg

Put carrots, celery, and onion into blender container. Cover with cold water. Cover; blend at medium speed just until chopped. Drain thoroughly in colander; reserve liquid. Heat butter in heavy saucepan. Add vegetables and cook over medium heat, stirring occasionally, until onion is golden. Add 1 can broth and 1 can reserved liquid; simmer about 8 minutes, or until vegetables are tender. Put mixture into blender container. Cover; blend at low speed until puréed. Pour into saucepan. Add remaining can of broth, another can of reserved liquid, farina, salt, pepper, and nutmeg. Simmer, stirring occasionally, for 20 minutes.

Chicken Corn Chowder

Makes about 4 servings

   2 cups water
   1 envelope Lipton® Chicken Noodle Recipe Soup
      Mix with Diced White Chicken Meat
   1 can (8½ ounces) cream-style corn
   ½ cup milk

In medium saucepan, bring water to a boil; stir in Lipton Chicken Noodle Recipe Soup Mix. Simmer covered 10 minutes. Stir in corn and milk and heat through, but do not boil.

Mushroom Bisque

Makes 6 servings

   6 tablespoons butter or margarine
   1 small onion, finely chopped
   1 pound mushrooms, finely chopped
   4 tablespoons flour
   3 cups chicken broth
   1 cup whipping cream
   ⅔ cup Seven Seas® Buttermilk Recipe Country
      Spice™ Dressing
      Pinch Cayenne pepper
   ½ teaspoon salt
      Sherry
      Chopped parsley

Melt 2 tablespoons butter and sauté onions over medium heat. Add dressing, then flour, and cook several minutes. In another pan, melt 4 tablespoons butter and add mushrooms; cover pan and lower heat for 5 minutes. Remove cover and raise heat to evaporate juices. Combine mushrooms with flour-butter mixture. Add broth, dressing, cream, salt, and Cayenne. Cook several minutes longer. Add sherry just before serving and garnish with chopped parsley.

Mushroom Soup Supreme

Makes 6 servings

- ¼ cup butter or margarine
- ½ pound mushrooms, sliced
- 2 cups chicken broth, or 2 chicken bouillon cubes dissolved in 2 cups hot water
- 2 eggs
- 1 cup light cream
- ¼ teaspoon salt
- ⅛ teaspoon pepper
- 2 tablespoons dry sherry (optional)

Heat butter in skillet. Add mushrooms and cook over medium heat, stirring occasionally, for 5 minutes. Set aside 6 slices for garnish. Put chicken broth and remaining mushrooms into blender container. Cover; blend at medium speed just until mushrooms are chopped. Add eggs; cover; blend at medium speed for 2 seconds. Pour into saucepan. Add cream, salt, and pepper. Stir over low heat until hot and slightly thickened. Remove from heat and stir in sherry, if desired. Garnish each serving with a mushroom slice.

Q. *I always peel carrots, but the other day I remembered that my grandmother used to scrape them. Which is best?*

A. The point is to remove as little of the carrot as possible. If you peel them with a knife, you're cutting away too much; peel with a swivel-blade vegetable parer, taking off as thin as possible an amount. If Grandmother scraped with a knife, she probably got too much, too. To scrape, use a wire brush or a clean metal pot sponge; once over lightly does it. Scraping by this method usually removes the least amount of carrot.

Creamy Mushroom Noodle Soup

Makes about 4 servings

- 2 tablespoons butter or margarine
- 1 can (4 ounces) sliced mushrooms, drained
- 1 envelope Lipton® Ring-O-Noodle Recipe Soup Mix with Real Chicken Broth
- 3 tablespoons all-purpose flour
- 3 cups water
- 1 cup milk

In medium saucepan, melt butter and cook mushrooms until tender. Blend in Lipton Ring-O-Noodle Recipe Soup Mix, flour, and water. Bring to a boil, then simmer covered 7 minutes; stir in milk; heat through, but do not boil.

French Onion Soup

Makes about 4 servings

- 1 envelope Lipton® Onion Recipe Soup Mix
- ¼ cup white wine
- ½ pound Swiss cheese, cubed
- 6 thin slices French bread, toasted
- ½ cup grated Parmesan cheese
- 1 tablespoon butter or margarine, melted

Preheat oven to 400°F. Prepare Lipton Onion Recipe Soup Mix according to package directions. Stir in wine. Pour soup into individual soup crocks or a 1¼-quart casserole and add cheese cubes. Top each serving with bread, sprinkle with Parmesan cheese, and drizzle with butter. Bake 7 minutes or until cheese is lightly browned.

Easy Onion Soup

Makes 6 servings

- 6 large yellow onions, thinly sliced
- ½ cup butter
- 2 cans (10½ ounces each) Campbell's Condensed Beef Broth
- 1 soup can water
- 1 soup can dry white wine
- 6 slices toasted French bread, about 1 inch thick
- ¾ cup grated Parmesan and gruyère cheese (freshly grated, if possible)

Sauté onions in butter until lightly browned. Add broth, water, and wine. Simmer until onions are tender. Spoon soup into earthenware or other oven-proof bowl. Top each serving with toasted French bread. Sprinkle with grated Parmesan and gruyère cheese. Broil until cheese is melted and golden brown.

Make-a-Meal Soup (page 48). Photograph was provided by Hunt-Wesson Foods, Inc.; photography by Tom Kelley Studios

All-You-Want Antipasto Salad (page 65); Fish Rolls with Vegetables and Clam Sauce (page 76); Hearty Sausage and Vegetable Soup (page 49). Courtesy of Progresso Quality Foods

Springtime Pea Soup

Makes 4 servings

    1 package (10 ounces) frozen peas
    1 cup chicken broth
    1 large lettuce leaf, torn into 4 pieces
    1 tablespoon minced onion
    ½ teaspoon salt
    ¼ teaspoon white pepper
    ⅛ teaspoon ground cardamom
    1 cup light or heavy cream

Break up frozen peas and place in blender container. Add broth, lettuce, onion, and seasonings. Cover and process at medium speed for 1 minute. Add cream and process at low speed 20 seconds. Chill at least 2 hours.

Split Pea Soup

Makes 12 servings

    2 cups split peas
    2 quarts water
      Ham bone
    2 medium onions, cut up
    2 medium carrots, pared and cut up
    2 stalks celery, cut up
    1 clove garlic, halved
    1 bay leaf
    2 teaspoons salt
    ¼ teaspoon pepper
    ¼ teaspoon dried thyme
      Croutons (optional)

Rinse and sort peas. Place in large saucepan with remaining ingredients except croutons. Heat to boiling; reduce heat; simmer covered for 2½ hours. Remove ham bone and bay leaf. Remove any meat from ham bone; cube and reserve; discard bone. Pour half the soup into blender container. Cover; blend at low speed until puréed. Pour into bowl. Repeat process with remaining soup. Return all soup to saucepan. Add ham pieces; heat to simmering. Garnish with croutons if desired.

Basque Potato Soup

Makes 6 servings

    1 egg
    ¼ cup packaged dry bread crumbs
    1 pound bulk sausage, crumbled
    1 tablespoon salad oil
    1 cup chopped onion
    ⅔ cup chopped green pepper
    1 clove garlic, minced
    2 cups sliced celery
    2 cups shredded cabbage
    1 cup sliced carrots
    2 cans (10½ ounces each) condensed beef broth
    1 can (1 pound) tomatoes
    6 cups water
    1 bay leaf
    1 tablespoon salt
    ½ teaspoon liquid pepper sauce
    3 cups cubed, pared Idaho® Potatoes

Beat together egg and bread crumbs in medium bowl; mix in sausage. Form into 1-inch balls. Heat oil in large, heavy kettle; brown meatballs over medium heat, remove and reserve. Add onion, green pepper and garlic to kettle; cook until onion is tender. Add remaining ingredients except potatoes. Return meatballs to kettle. Cover, cook 1½ hours. Add potatoes; cook covered 20 minutes longer or until potatoes are tender.

Vichyssoise

Makes 6 servings

    2 tablespoons butter or margarine
    5 leeks, white parts only, sliced ¼ inch thick, or
        1 medium onion, sliced
    2 cups pared and sliced potatoes
    2 cups chicken broth, or 2 chicken bouillon cubes
        dissolved in 2 cups hot water
    ¾ teaspoon salt
    ¼ teaspoon pepper
    1 cup milk
    ¾ cup heavy cream
      Chopped chives

Heat butter in skillet. Add leeks; cook over medium heat, stirring occasionally, until tender but not brown. Add potatoes, broth, salt, and pepper. Bring to a boil; reduce heat; simmer until potatoes are very tender. Pour half the mixture into blender container. Cover; blend at high speed until smooth. Empty into bowl. Repeat process with remaining soup. Return all soup to saucepan. Add milk; heat just to boiling. Stir in cream. Chill. Garnish with chopped chives.

Storing Vegetables

Asparagus: Preferably, buy asparagus the day you're going to cook it. Store it unwashed in the refrigerator, in a covered container or plastic bag. It will keep up to 4 days, but lose a little of its *joie de vivre* with each passing day.

Beans: Shelled limas should be cooked the day they are purchased to be certain of best flavor—their keeping qualities leave a good deal to be desired. Limas and favas and soybeans in the pod, and green and wax beans should be stored in the refrigerator in a plastic bag or moistureproof covered container. Plan to use them as soon after buying as possible, for they toughen with each passing day; in any case, 3 days' storage should be the maximum. Plan to use them up within 3 days once they're cooked, too.

Broccoli: Store in the vegetable crisper, or in a closed plastic bag, in the refrigerator. Don't plan on keeping broccoli, raw or after it's been cooked, for more than 4 days.

Cabbage: Store in the refrigerator crisper, or in a closed plastic bag, up to 8 days. If there are any wilted leaves, pluck them off before storing the cabbage. Refrigerate cooked cabbage, covered, up to 4 days.

Carrots: If the tops are still in place, remove them. Refrigerate, in plastic bags or wrapped in foil, preferably in the refrigerator's vegetable crisper. up to 4 weeks. Cooked carrots—covered and refrigerated—keep up to 5 days.

Celery: Keep celery cool and dry, in a covered container, in a closed-up plastic bag or closely wrapped in foil; store leaves and stalk separately, but do not cut off the root end—celery keeps better with it in place. Well stored, it will keep 8 days, often as long as 2 weeks. Freshen in ice water celery that has begun to grow limp. Cooked celery, covered and refrigerated, will keep up to 5 days.

Corn: In a word, don't store. If at all possible, cook and serve fresh corn immediately. At any rate, don't keep it overnight if you truly enjoy the vegetable at its best. Store briefly in the refrigerator; do not strip off husks and silk until just before cooking.

Cooked corn (off the cob) can be stored in the refrigerator, closely covered, up to 3 days.

Eggplant: Refrigerate—eggplants like high humidity—up to 6 weeks in the raw state. Cooked, refrigerate, tightly covered, up to 5 days.

Mushrooms: Mushrooms bought loose or in a paper carton can be stored in the refrigerator as is if you're going to use them on the day of purchase. If you wish to hold them up to 5 days, take a little more care: spread the mushrooms out on a nonmetal platter or tray in a single layer, cover with dampened paper towels and refrigerate. Store cooked mushrooms in a tightly covered container, in the refrigerator, up to 3 days.

Onions: Dry onions need a cool, well-ventilated place, spread in a single layer, where moisture will not get to them; they need not be refrigerated, and may be stored up to 4 weeks under optimum conditions. Trim the tops (only the wilted ends) and roots of leeks and scallions; enclose tightly in a plastic bag and refrigerate up to 3 weeks. Place cut chives in a small water-filled glass, as if they were a bouquet, and enclose glass and all in an airtight plastic bag; refrigerate up to 2 weeks. Refrigerate cooked onions of all kinds in a tightly covered container up to 5 days.

Peas: Do not shell peas until shortly before you are going to cook them. Store, unshelled, in the refrigerator up to 5 days. After cooking, refrigerate in a covered container up to 5 days. Store uncooked split dried peas on a cool, dry kitchen shelf up to 8 months.

Peppers: Refrigerate, covered or in a plastic bag, up to 5 days; cooked, refrigerate in a covered container 1 or 2 days.

Potatoes: Potatoes should not be refrigerated. On the other hand, their best keeping temperature is between 45° and 50°F. and few of our kitchens are that cold. Store in the coolest possible place—a sheltered but unheated back entryway is ideal. If you have no such storage place, don't buy more potatoes than you'll use in a week's time. Avoid long exposure to light—that's what gives them the green tinge.

Spinach: In the refrigerator, in a plastic bag, raw spinach can be stored up to 5 days. Cooked spinach, in a covered container, can be refrigerated up to 5 days as well.

Tomatoes: If fully ripe, store in the vegetable crisper of the refrigerator. If mature but not ripe, store at room temperature—60° to 70°F.—until ripe. Do not try to ripen tomatoes in sunlight, which inhibits color and flavor development. The best method is to put several together in a paper bag. Don't close it tightly—and don't forget about them! Ripe tomatoes will keeep, refrigerated, up to 5 days.

Easy Potato Soup

Makes 6 to 8 servings

 1 onion, sliced
 ½ cup minced celery
 1 cup diced smoked ham
   Water
 2 cans (10½ ounces each) Campbell's Condensed
     Cream of Potato Soup
 1½ cups milk
 1½ cups light cream
 1 tablespoon Worcestershire sauce
   Cayenne
   Salt
   Scallions or chives

In a large saucepan, combine onion, celery, and ham. Add water to cover. Simmer covered until vegetables are tender. Press mixture through a sieve or whirl in a blender. Return to saucepan and add remaining ingredients. Season to taste with Cayenne and salt. Heat until soup starts to bubble. Serve hot or icy cold, sprinkled with finely chopped scallions or chives.

Pumpkin Soup

Makes 4 to 6 servings

 2 cups chicken broth, or 2 chicken bouillon cubes
     dissolved in 2 cups hot water
 ½ green pepper, seeded and cut up
 1 small onion, cut up
 1 sprig parsley
 ¼ teaspoon dried thyme
 1 can (16 ounces) pumpkin
 1 tablespoon all-purpose flour
 2 tablespoons butter or margarine
 1 cup milk
 1 teaspoon sugar
 ½ teaspoon ground nutmeg
 ½ teaspoon salt

Put 1 cup chicken broth, green pepper, onion, parsley, and thyme into blender container. Cover; blend at medium speed until vegetables are coarsely chopped. Pour into saucepan; simmer 5 minutes. Return mixture to blender container; add pumpkin and flour. Cover; blend at high speed until smooth. Pour into saucepan; stir in remaining 1 cup chicken broth and remaining ingredients. Heat to boiling, stirring often; simmer 3 minutes.

Hot Borscht (page 52). Lea & Perrins

Fresh Tomato Soup

Makes 4 servings

 1 onion, finely chopped
 ¼ cup butter or margarine
 2 tablespoons olive oil
 2 pounds ripe tomatoes, cored and coarsely diced
 1 can (10¾ ounces) condensed chicken broth,
     undiluted
 2 tablespoons chopped fresh basil or 1 teaspoon
     dry basil
 2 teaspoons chopped fresh thyme or ½ teaspoon
     dry thyme
 2 teaspoons sugar
 2 tablespoons cornstarch
 ½ cup half and half or heavy cream (optional)
   Salt and freshly ground pepper to taste

Sauté onion in butter and oil until onion is transparent. Add tomatoes, chicken broth, basil, thyme, and sugar. Heat to boiling. Reduce heat, cover, and simmer 30 minutes. Press soup through fine sieve. Discard seeds and skin. Mix cornstarch and 3 tablespoons water until smooth. Stir into soup. Heat to boiling. Boil 1 minute. Stir in half and half, season with salt and pepper, and serve.

This recipe was provided by the makers of Saran Wrap™ brand plastic film.

Mushroom Bisque (page 53). Seven Seas®/Phil Kretchmar

Grandmother's Cream of Tomato

Makes 6 servings

  1 **can (28 ounces) tomatoes**
  4 **sprigs parsley**
  1 **small onion, cut up**
  1 **stalk celery, cut up**
  3 **tablespoons all-purpose flour**
  2 **teaspoons brown sugar**
  1 **teaspoon salt**
  ½ **teaspoon dried basil**
  ⅛ **teaspoon pepper**
  2 **tablespoons butter or margarine**
  2 **cups milk**
    Croutons or parsley sprigs (optional)

Put tomatoes with their liquid, parsley, onion, celery, flour, brown sugar, salt, basil, and pepper into blender container. Cover; blend at high speed until smooth. Heat butter in saucepan. Stir in tomato mixture gradually. Cook over medium heat, stirring constantly, until mixture comes to a boil. Add milk slowly; heat gently just until simmering. Garnish with croutons or parsley if desired.

Sorrel Soup

Makes 4 to 6 servings

  1 **pound sorrel or ½ pound sorrel and ½ pound**
    spinach
  1 **teaspoon salt**
    White of 1 egg, beaten until foamy (optional)
  ½ **cucumber, diced**
  4 **scallions, chopped**
  1 **hard-cooked egg**
    Cream or sour cream (optional)

Wash sorrel leaves and drain. Discard stems, retaining half inch, if desired. Bring 6 cups water to a boil, add sorrel and salt and cook for 3 minutes. Remove leaves. Chop or put in a blender with a small amount of the liquid. Do not chop too fine. Return leaves to liquid. Chill and stir in the beaten white of egg if it is being used. Add cucumber, scallions, and hard-cooked egg put through a coarse strainer. Serve with sweet or sour cream, if desired.

How to Prepare Leeks

Cut off a portion of the green end so that about 5 inches remain; strip off the outside leaves and cut off the root end. Because the convolutions of leeks offer many hiding places for dirt and sand, they must be thoroughly washed, either under running water (turn them so that water runs into them) or in several changes of cold water.

To be served either hot or cold, leeks need only a relatively brief cooking time, 15 to 20 minutes. Cook in boiling salted water or braise in a small amount of chicken or beef stock or bouillon. Drain well and serve at once, or refrigerate to serve cold. Count on two to four leeks per serving, depending on their size.

Hot leeks may be simply dressed with butter or lemon butter. Or braise the vegetable (on top of the stove or in the oven) in bouillon with a bay leaf and a little thyme, and serve with a sour-cream or a mushroom sauce, or with a liberal sprinkling of butter-browned bread crumbs. Or serve, as you might asparagus, with hollandaise sauce or a white sauce with hard-cooked eggs.

Leeks in the soup: Flemish-style leek soup combines the vegetable with sorrel, chervil, and winter savory for flavoring, and with potatoes; the soup is cooked up to 3 hours, by which time the potatoes will have disintegrated into the water to form a thick, creamy mixture. French-style leek soup calls for cooking cut-up leeks slowly in hot butter, adding flour and hot milk; the whole business is puréed through a sieve, then cream is added and the soup reheated. Scotch-style leek soup, called Cock-a-leekie, cooks the leeks in chicken broth thickened with oatmeal. Welsh-style cooks cut-up leeks and an onion in butter, then adds them to partially cooked potatoes, and continues cooking until the potatoes are done; the mixture is sieved and then stirred into beaten egg yolks in a soup tureen, along with a small amount of heavy cream.

Tomato-Celery Soup

Makes 2 to 3 servings

  1 **cup finely chopped celery**
  2 **tablespoons butter or margarine**
  1 **can (10¾ ounces) Campbell's Condensed**
    Tomato Soup
  1 **cup milk**
    Croutons (optional)

In saucepan, cook celery in butter until tender. Stir in soup and milk. Heat, stirring occasionally. Serve with croutons, if desired.

Watercress Soup

Makes 6 servings
- ½ cup butter
- ½ cup finely chopped leeks
- 1 can (10½ ounces) Campbell's Condensed Cream of Potato Soup
- 1 can (10½ ounces) Campbell's Condensed Chicken Broth
- 1 cup milk
- 1 cup light cream
- 1 tablespoon chopped parsley
- 1 bunch watercress, stems removed and finely chopped

Heat butter and sauté leeks until tender but not brown. Add soups, milk, cream, parsley, and watercress. Simmer for 5 minutes. Serve hot.

Chilled Cream of Watercress Soup

Makes 8 servings
- 2 tablespoons butter or margarine
- 1 small onion, sliced
- 3 tablespoons all-purpose flour
- 1 teaspoon salt
- ¼ teaspoon pepper
- 2 cans (13¾ ounces each) chicken broth
- 4 cups watercress, coarse stems removed
- 1 cup heavy cream
    Watercress sprigs

Heat butter in large saucepan. Add onion and cook over medium heat, stirring occasionally, until golden. Remove from heat. Blend in flour, salt, and pepper. Gradually stir in chicken broth. Cook, stirring constantly, until mixture thickens and comes to a boil. Add watercress and simmer 5 minutes. Pour half of watercress mixture into blender container. Cover; blend at high speed until smooth but still slightly flecked with green. Pour into large bowl. Repeat process with remaining watercress mixture. Add cream. Cover and chill thoroughly. To serve, garnish with additional watercress.

Chilled Zucchini Soup

Makes about 4 cups
- 1 can (13¾ ounces) chicken broth
- 3 medium zucchini, sliced
- 2 medium onions, chopped
- 1 clove garlic, sliced
- ¼ teaspoon salt
- 1 cup Hellmann's or Best Foods Real Mayonnaise
- 1 teaspoon lemon juice
- ¼ teaspoon ground nutmeg
    Lemon slices

Place first 5 ingredients in 3-quart saucepan. Bring to boil over high heat. Reduce heat to low, and simmer covered 10 minutes, or until vegetables are tender; cool. Place half at a time in blender container; cover. Blend until uniform. Pour into large bowl. Stir in remaining ingredients. Cover; chill overnight. Garnish with lemon slices.

A Little Something Extra

Before you send soup—particularly smooth soups such as creams and broths—to the table, add a bit of garnish for both eye- and appetite-appeal. Nothing in the house? Of course you have—just look around you. A whole pretzel will float on top of the soup. So will packaged croutons. So will "soup nuts," those little puffs of chou paste that you can buy packaged or make at home. Try a drift of snipped chives or parsley across a cold soup. Float a slice of lemon on black bean soup, or sprinkle with chopped hard-cooked egg mixed with minced green onion. Avocado slices make a handsome garnish. So does a dollop of cream, either sour or unsweetened whipped, topped with a blush of paprika. Summer soups take kindly to a little snipped fresh herb—thyme, sage, basil, and savory are favorites. Winter soups go well when dressed with a generous spoonful of shredded cheese. For crunch, try chopped nuts, canned French fried onion, chow-mein noodles. Or shape thin slices of raw vegetable, such as carrot or turnip, with tiny canapé cutters. Popcorn makes a handsome and delicious garnish.

To give a soup more substance, garnish with small meatballs or sausage balls, or slices of sausage, or slivers of leftover ham or chicken, or crumbled crisp bacon. To turn a meal-starter soup into a main dish, add rice or pasta for extra substance, or follow the good Mexican example and slip a poached egg into the serving dish. Or do it the French way. Ladle soup into ovenproof bowls. On each serving, float a slice of toasted, buttered bread, liberally sprinkled with shredded cheese. Run under the broiler for a few moments, then serve at once.

Green—and Glorious

Salads are not everyone's favorite food, but they can be when approached with a fresh eye and a lot of bright, innovative ideas.

Oriental Chicken Salad

Makes 6 servings

- ¾ cup Ocean Spray Cranorange Cranberry Orange Sauce
- 1 tablespoon soy sauce
- ½ teaspoon ginger
- ¾ teaspoon red wine vinegar
- 2 cups cooked diced chicken
- ½ cup blanched, halved snow peas
- 1 cup thinly sliced Chinese cabbage
- ¼ cup very thinly sliced carrots
- ¼ cup very thinly sliced red pepper
- 2 tablespoons sliced scallions

In a bowl, combine cranberry orange sauce, soy sauce, ginger, and vinegar. Cover and chill. In a large bowl, toss together remaining ingredients. Serve with dressing.

German Potato Salad

Makes 6 servings

- 6 medium potatoes
- 5 tablespoons butter or margarine
- 2 knockwurst, cut in half and sliced
- 1 medium onion, sliced
- 2 tablespoons flour
- ¾ cup red wine vinegar
- ¾ cup apple juice
- 1½ teaspoons sugar
- ¼ teaspoon pepper

In medium kettle, boil potatoes with skins on until done. Meanwhile, in large skillet, melt 2 tablespoons butter. Add knockwurst and sauté until brown. Stir in onion and cook until just tender. Remove from skillet. Melt remaining 3 tablespoons butter in skillet; stir in flour. Remove from heat and beat in vinegar and apple juice. Stir in sugar and pepper. Return to heat and cook, stirring until thickened. Add knockwurst and onions; cover and remove from heat.

When potatoes are cooked, peel and slice into sauce. Stir gently to coat with sauce and heat through. Serve immediately.

French/American Vegetable Salad

Makes 6 servings

- ½ cup Ocean Spray Jellied Cranberry Sauce
- ½ cup yogurt
- 1 small clove garlic, crushed
- 2 tablespoons chopped parsley
- ⅓ cup chopped celery
- 1 tablespoon catsup
- ¼ to ½ head Romaine leaves
- 4 tomatoes, cut into wedges
- 1½ pounds whole asparagus, cooked and chilled
- ½ avocado cut into wedges
- 1 can (8 ounces) artichoke hearts

In a bowl, beat jellied cranberry sauce with wire whisk until smooth. Stir in yogurt, garlic, parsley, celery, and catsup. Cover and chill.

Arrange vegetables on romaine leaves. Drizzle dressing over vegetables just before serving.

Cranberry Waldorf Mold

Makes 8 servings

- 1 package (12 ounces) fresh cranberries
- ⅔ cup sugar
- 1 envelope unflavored gelatin
- 1 cup freshly squeezed orange juice
- 1 small apple, pared, cored, and chopped (1 cup)
- ½ cup chopped celery
- ½ cup chopped pecans or walnuts

Wash cranberries; drain; remove stems. In food processor using coarse blade, or with a heavy chopping knife, chop cranberries until fine. In large bowl, combine cranberries and sugar; let stand 15 minutes, stirring occasionally. Sprinkle gelatin over orange juice in small saucepan; let stand 1 minute. Stir over medium heat until gelatin is completely dissolved, about 1 minute. Add gelatin mixture, apple, celery, and nuts to cranberries; mix well. Turn into oiled, 1-quart mold. Refrigerate until firm, about 3 to 4 hours.

French/American Vegetable Salad; Oriental Chicken Salad; German Potato Salad. Ocean Spray Cranberries

Lebanese Tossed Salad

Makes 4 servings

⅓ cup olive oil
2 tablespoons lemon juice
1 clove garlic, minced
½ teaspoon salt
  Few drops hot pepper sauce
1 pita bread or 4 very thin slices French bread
1 small cucumber
2 cups lightly packed torn lettuce or spinach
½ cup sliced scallions
½ cup chopped parsley
¼ cup Sun-Maid® Zante Currants
¼ cup chopped mint
2 medium-size tomatoes, diced

In a small bowl or a jar with a light lid, combine the oil, lemon juice, garlic, salt, and hot pepper sauce. Separate the pita bread into 2 slices or layers. Toast and break into 1-inch pieces for croutons.

Cut the cucumber in half lengthwise and scoop out the seeds with the tip of a spoon. Thinly slice the cucumber and combine with the remaining ingredients, except the tomatoes, in a salad bowl. Toss with the dressing and serve garnished with the croutons and tomatoes.

Riviera Salad

Makes 4 servings

6 tablespoons cooking oil
2 tablespoons vinegar
1 teaspoon prepared mustard
½ teaspoon thyme
¼ teaspoon salt
⅛ teaspoon pepper
1 clove garlic, minced
1 pound potatoes (3 medium)
½ pound fresh green beans
1 small red onion, thinly sliced
1 quart bite-size lettuce pieces
1 can (12 ounces) SPAM®, cubed
1 can (3½ ounces) black olives, drained

Combine cooking oil, vinegar, mustard, thyme, salt, pepper, and garlic; mix well; reserve. Cook unpeeled potatoes until tender; drain. Cool to room temperature; peel and cube. Cut beans into 1-inch lengths; cook until tender-crisp; drain and cool to room temperature. Combine potatoes, green beans, and onion; cover and refrigerate until cold. Before serving, place lettuce in salad bowl; top with vegetable mixture. Pile SPAM® in center; sprinkle olives over top. Pour on reserved dressing; toss well.

Potato Salad

Makes 2 quarts

2 pounds potatoes (6 medium)
1 can (12 ounces) SPAM®, cubed
½ cup cooked diced carrots
½ cup frozen peas, thawed
½ cup chopped dill pickles
¼ cup finely chopped onion
¾ cup mayonnaise
2 tablespoons dill pickle liquid
  Salt and pepper to taste

Cook unpeeled potatoes in boiling salted water until tender; drain. Cool slightly; peel. Cool to room temperature; cut into ½-inch cubes. Combine SPAM® with potatoes in large bowl. Gently mix in carrots, peas, pickles, and onion. Stir together mayonnaise and pickle liquid; gently stir into SPAM® mixture. Season to taste with salt and pepper. Cover and refrigerate until serving time, at least 1 hour.

A Dab of This, a Dab of That

Leftover vegetables—two tablespoons of green beans, one cold cob of corn, a quarter cup of diced carrots—can either take up precious refrigerator space or be a hoard that promises something very good later in the week, depending on how you view them. You can add them to heated-up canned soup for lunch, for instance. Or combine them with another vegetable at dinnertime. Or, best of all, stockpile vegetable leftovers for Russian Salad. For this, combine leftover cooked vegetables in any variety the refrigerator has to offer with thin-sliced celery for crunch, pressed garlic or garlic juice for zipped-up flavor, a squirt of lemon juice for freshness, salt and pepper to taste. Dress with enough mayonnaise to bind, or half-and-half mayonnaise and sour cream if calories don't count or plain yogurt if they do. Chopped nuts of any kind are a good addition, too. Funny thing about this salad: the English call it French Salad, the French call it Italian Salad, the Italians call it Russian Salad. And the Russians? Who knows!

All-You-Want Antipasto Salad

Makes 8 servings

⅓ cup olive oil
3 tablespoons red wine vinegar
½ teaspoon Italian seasoning, crushed
½ teaspoon salt
¼ teaspoon garlic powder
  Dash ground black pepper
1 can (10½ ounces) red kidney beans, drained
1 can (10½ ounces) chick-peas, drained
  Lettuce leaves
4 ounces sliced provolone cheese, cut in ½-inch
  strips
4 ounces sliced salami, rolled
1 jar (7¼ ounces) roasted red peppers, drained
1 jar (9 ounces) Tuscan peppers, drained
1 jar (3¾ ounces) marinated artichokes, drained
  Radish roses

Combine oil, vinegar, Italian seasoning, salt, garlic powder, and black pepper. Pour over kidney beans and chick-peas (either mixed together or in separate bowls); mix lightly. Cover and refrigerate at least 2 hours. Just before serving, line a 2½-quart bowl with lettuce leaves. With a slotted spoon remove beans (reserving dressing) and place on lettuce. Arrange cheese, salami, peppers, artichokes, and radishes in any desired pattern, Serve with reserved dressing.

Bean Salad

Makes 6 to 8 servings

¼ cup olive oil
2 tablespoons wine vinegar
2 tablespoons finely chopped onion
½ teaspoon salt
½ teaspoon sugar
¼ teaspoon dry mustard
⅛ teaspoon ground black pepper
1 can (19 ounces) cannellini (white kidney) beans
1 can (19 ounces) chick-peas (ceci)
1 quart torn mixed salad greens
¼ cup roasted peppers, cut in slivers
  Parmesan cheese, grated (optional)

In a small measuring cup, combine oil, vinegar, onion, salt, sugar, mustard, and black pepper; mix well and set aside. Drain beans and chick-peas thoroughly. Place in separate bowls; pour half of the oil mixture over each bowl of beans; mix well. Cover and refrigerate for at least 1 hour. To serve, place salad greens in bowl. Arrange beans in alternate clusters on the greens; garnish with roasted peppers. Toss just before serving, sprinkling lightly with oil, vinegar, and grated Parmesan cheese, if desired.

Dressed-up Dining

Perhaps you are one of those people who feel a meal is not a meal without a salad. You can add a salad to almost any menu that does not call for one, anything from sliced tomatoes with a good dressing through a wedge of lettuce nicely dressed or a tossed green salad to a refreshing fruit salad that augments, or doubles for, dessert. Here are salad dressings of several kinds, with comments on what they dress best.

French Dressing

Makes about ½ cup dressing

6 tablespoons olive oil, divided
2 tablespoons red or white vinegar or lemon
  juice, divided
¼ teaspoon salt
¼ teaspoon pepper
1 teaspoon dry mustard (optional)
1 peeled garlic clove (optional)

In a small bowl, combine 1 tablespoon olive oil, 1 tablespoon vinegar or lemon juice, salt, pepper, and mustard, if desired. Beat with a fork until well combined. Add 2 tablespoons olive oil and beat again. Add 1 tablespoon vinegar or lemon juice and 3 tablespoons olive oil. Add garlic, if desired. Place the dressing in a jar, well covered, and refrigerate. Shake well before using.

Blue Cheese Dressing

Into ½ cup of French Dressing (see above), beat 3 tablespoons crumbled blue cheese. Serve on mixed greens or lettuce wedge.

Thousand Island Dressing

Makes about 1 cup dressing

1 cup mayonnaise
3 tablespoons catsup
½ teaspoon Worcestershire sauce
2 tablespoons grated onion
2 tablespoons sweet pickle relish, well drained
2 chopped hard-cooked eggs
1 tablespoon snipped parsley

Into mayonnnaise, beat the remaining ingredients.
Dresses up a plain wedge of lettuce; fine with shrimp or egg dishes of any kind.

Salade Niçoise

Makes 2 servings

- 1 small head Bibb lettuce
- 1 cup cooked new potatoes, cooled and quartered
- 1 cup steamed green beans, cooled
- 1 cup Vinaigrette or Italian Dressing (see index)
- 1 can (6½ ounces) tuna fish, flaked
- 2 small ripe tomatoes, cut in wedges
- 2 hard-cooked eggs, quartered
- 2 anchovy fillets

Arrange lettuce on a serving platter. Scatter potatoes over half the platter. Toss green beans with half the dressing and scatter over other half of the platter. Mound tuna in the center of the platter. Place tomato wedges and egg quarters around the edges of the platter. Garnish with anchovies. Pass the remaining dressing.

Variations

Try adding any of the following to the salad: sliced green pepper, onion rings, capers, snipped parsley or other fresh herb, green or black olives, chopped celery.

Tuna and Fried Peppers

Makes 8 appetizers

- 1 jar (6 ounces) sweet fried peppers and onions
- 1 can (7 ounces) tuna, drained and flaked
- 3 tablespoons finely chopped onion
- 3 tablespoons chopped parsley
- 2 teaspoons wine vinegar
- ⅛ teaspoon ground black pepper
  Lettuce leaves
  Oil-cured olives (optional)

In a medium bowl, combine all ingredients except lettuce and olives. Arrange lettuce leaves on a platter to form a cup; fill with tuna-and-pepper mixture. Serve with oil-cured olives, if desired.

Q. *I'm sure my mother used to ripen green tomatoes by setting them on the windowsill, but when I do it they rot before they ripen. What am I doing wrong?*

A. You're doing wrong the same thing your mother did—you're putting them on the windowsill. (You've probably forgotten that besides putting them on the windowsill she also often said, "Pshaw! These tomatoes are no good.") Put them in a bag to ripen. As with other fruit, several will ripen more readily than a single fruit. A plastic bag is fine, but don't put it into direct light, and don't close it airtight. The USDA suggests that the best way of all is to give tomatoes—and peaches, pears, and any other fruit you need to ripen—a friend to help them: a very ripe apple. Ripe apples give off ethylene, a gas that helps unripe fruit to ripen. Be sure that the container or bag is not tightly closed, because that will cause a too-high concentration of carbon dioxide, and retard ripening; also, it may cause too high a humidity, which will encourage spoilage. If you wish tomatoes to ripen very slowly, refrigerate them in their air-circulating bag, without the apple.

Salade Niçoise.

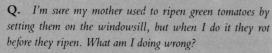

Marinated Vegetable Kebabs, Italiano (page 25); Italian Beef Stew (page 76); Bean Salad (page 65); Tuna and Fried Peppers.
Courtesy of Progresso Quality Foods

Hot Potato Salad

Makes 6 servings

- 2½ pounds potatoes
- ½ cup sliced radishes
- ½ cup chopped parsley
- ¼ cup Hormel Bacon Bits
- ¾ teaspoon celery seed
- ½ cup chopped onions
- 2 tablespoons cooking oil
- 1 tablespoon all-purpose flour
- ¾ teaspoon salt
- ⅛ teaspoon pepper
- ½ cup water
- ¾ cup vinegar
- 2 tablespoons sugar

Cook unpeeled potatoes in small amount of boiling salted water until tender; drain. Cool slightly; peel. Dice potatoes; combine with radishes, parsley, bacon, and celery seed. In small saucepan, sauté onions in oil until transparent; blend in flour, salt, and pepper. Add water, vinegar, and sugar; cook over medium heat, stirring until mixture thickens and boils. Pour hot sauce over potato mixture; stir gently to mix well. Serve warm.

Hearty Supper Salad

Makes 4 to 6 servings

- 1 small head iceberg lettuce, torn into pieces
- 2 cups cut-up cooked chicken
- 2 medium tomatoes, quartered
- 1 small cucumber, sliced
- 1 cup sliced celery
- 1 cup Lipton California Dip (see index)
- ¼ cup lemon juice
- 2 teaspoons sugar

In salad bowl, arrange lettuce, chicken, tomatoes, cucumber, and celery; chill. Just before serving, toss with Lipton California Dip blended with lemon juice and sugar.

Variations

Substitute ham, pork, beef, turkey, or any combination to your taste for the chicken.

Vinaigrette Plus

For a tossed green salad, an oil-and-vinegar dressing suits most tastes. Here is an easy, untypical one to try: In a jar with a leakproof cover, combine ½ teaspoon garlic juice, a 2-inch strip of anchovy paste (from a tube), 3 tablespoons red wine vinegar, ¼ cup olive oil, ⅓ cup salad oil, and ¼ teaspoon coarsely ground pepper. This is particularly good on a salad made in part with a strong-flavored green, such as curly endive or radicchio, or used to dress a simple dish of alternating slices of mozzarella cheese and tomatoes.

Chef's Salad

Makes 4 servings

- 1 quart torn salad greens
- 1 tomato, coarsely chopped
- 1 can (6¾ ounces) Hormel Chunk Ham, drained and flaked
- 2 ounces Swiss cheese, cut in thin strips
- 1 can (6¾ ounces) Hormel Chunk Turkey, drained and flaked
- 1 hard-cooked egg, sliced
- ¼ cup pitted black olives, halved
- ⅓ cup Italian dressing

Place greens in shallow salad bowl. Sprinkle tomato around edges of bowl. Add a circle of ham, then a circle of cheese. Fill center with turkey. Top with egg slices; sprinkle olives over all. Just before serving, toss well with dressing.

Tomato Aspic

Makes 4 servings

- 1 envelope unflavored gelatin
- 2 cups tomato juice
- ¼ cup chopped onion
- 2 tablespoons snipped celery leaves
- 1 tablespoon light brown sugar
- ½ teaspoon salt
- 1 small bay leaf
- 2 whole cloves
- 1½ tablespoons lemon juice
- ½ cup finely chopped celery
- Homemade Russian Dressing (recipe follows)

Soften gelatin in ½ cup tomato juice. Mix 1½ cups tomato juice with onion, celery leaves, sugar, salt, bay leaf and cloves. Heat just to boiling; strain. Add gelatin and stir until dissolved. Stir in lemon juice. Chill until partially set. Add celery. Pour into a 3-cup mold. Chill until firm. Serve with Home-made Russian Dressing.

Homemade Russian Dressing

Makes about 1¼ cups dressing

- 1 cup mayonnaise
- 1 tablespoon horseradish, drained
- 1 teaspoon Worcestershire sauce
- ¼ cup chili sauce
- 1 teaspoon grated onion
- 3 tablespoons caviar (optional)

Into mayonnaise, stir in remaining ingredients until well blended. Chill.

Note: Use on cold vegetable salads or on chicken, fish, or shellfish—especially delicious on shrimp.

Javanese Bean Sprout Salad

Makes 4 to 6 servings

- **3 cups (6 ounces) bean sprouts**
- **⅓ cup Sun-Maid® Seedless Raisins**
- **¼ cup minced green pepper**
- **¼ cup minced red onion**
- **1 jar (2 ounces) sliced pimiento, drained**
- **¼ cup cider vinegar**
- **2 tablespoons peanut oil**
- **1 tablespoon soy sauce**
- **¼ teaspoon salt**
- **¼ teaspoon sugar**
- **½ cup dry-roasted peanuts, coarsely chopped**

Combine and toss the bean sprouts with the raisins, green pepper, onion, and pimiento. Mix the vinegar, oil, soy sauce, salt, and sugar and toss with the salad. Chill for 1 hour, tossing twice during that period. Sprinkle with the peanuts and serve.

Vegetable Wreath Tarte

Makes one 12-inch tarte

- **1 12-inch baked tarte or pie shell (see index or use your favorite short crust pastry recipe)**
- **1 pound ricotta cheese**
- **1 cup cream cheese**
- **1 tablespoon fines herbs (or your favorite mixture; a tarragon blend is also very nice)**
- **2 tablespoons prepared Dijon mustard**
- **Cauliflower (cut into flowerets)**
- **Carrots (cut into ovals)**
- **Snow peas (trimmed)**
- **Whole pimiento (cut as a bow)**
- **Glaze (recipe follows)**

Bake and cool tarte crust. Combine ricotta and cream cheeses, herbs, and mustard in food processor and blend until smooth. Spread cheese filling mixture evenly over inside of crust. Wash and blanch vegetables; pat dry. Starting at outer edge of crust, form a ring of cauliflowerets accented by half carrot ovals. Next, create a wreath with snow peas. Overlap peas end to end in 3 concentric circles. Fill center with carrot ovals. Place pimiento bow at top or bottom of snow pea wreath.

Carefully spoon cool glaze over all. Chill until firm. Cut into bite-size hors d'oeuvres. Stores well.

Glaze

- **1¼ cups chicken stock**
- **1 tablespoon unflavored gelatin**

In a small saucepan, dissolve gelatin into cold stock. Heat just to boiling. Cool in refrigerator until mixture just begins to gel, but pours smoothly.

Burgundy Crown Salad

Makes 6 servings

- **1 tablespoon blue cheese, crumbled**
- **1 clove crushed garlic**
- **¼ cup olive oil**
- **⅛ cup Paul Masson Burgundy**
- **Salt and pepper to taste**
- **1 bunch fresh spinach, rinsed, drained, and stemmed**
- **1 can (16 ounces) julienned beets, drained**

Mix the first 5 ingredients and set aside. Arrange spinach in serving bowl and crown with beets. Immediately before serving the salad, add Burgundy dressing and toss.

Botany Lesson

What is a tomato—a vegetable or a fruit? Fortunately, that's easier to answer than the thorny one about which came first, the chicken or the egg. The tomato is definitely, once and for all, a fruit. That we use it as a vegetable doesn't change its botanical classification. A fruit is the mature ovary of a flower; all fruits contain seeds. (They do, that is, when left as nature intended them. When man tampers and breeds a fruit without seeds, it's called a parthenocarpic fruit—but still a fruit, nonetheless.) Subdividing fruit classification further, a tomato is actually a berry, just as much so as a strawberry. Are all fruits berries, then? Not at all. An apple is a pome—a fleshy fruit all of whose seeds are in one area and are encapsulated. A peach and a cherry are both drupes—fruits with a single, central seed. But back to vegetables, and fruits used as vegetables. Other fruits that, as far as our kitchens are concerned, are treated as vegetables include cucumbers, avocados, squash, pumpkins, peppers, and eggplant. But don't conclude that all vegetables are really fruits in disguise. Brussels sprouts, for example, are buds. Kale and spinach, lettuce and cabbage are all leaves; so are most of the herbs we use in our kitchens, although there are some exceptions. Broccoli and cauliflower, at least the parts we eat, are flowers, and so are the delicate squash blossoms of Chinese cuisine. Class dismissed.

Tangy Ditalini Salad

Makes 4 to 6 servings

    1 cup (8-ounce container) plain yogurt
    2 tablespoons vegetable oil
    1 tablespoon tarragon-flavored vinegar
    2 tablespoons chopped onion
    1 tablespoon chopped fresh parsley
    ½ teaspoon salt
    ¼ teaspoon garlic powder
    ¼ teaspoon oregano
    ⅛ teaspoon white pepper
    1¾ cups (8 ounces) San Giorgio® Ditalini,
        uncooked
    2 cups chopped fresh raw cauliflower
    1 cup sliced carrots
    1 cup sliced celery

Place yogurt, oil, vinegar, onion, parsley, salt, garlic powder, oregano, and white pepper in food processor or blender container. Process or blend on high speed 2 minutes, or until smooth and creamy. Refrigerate at least 2 hours. Cook ditalini according to package directions; drain. Cool. (Rinse with cold water to cool quickly; drain well.) Combine drained ditalini, cauliflower, carrots, and celery in large bowl. Add dressing; toss lightly until all ingredients are well coated. Chill.

Tomato-Zucchini Orzo Salad

Makes 4 servings

    1¼ cups (8 ounces) San Giorgio® Orzo or Rosa
        Marina, uncooked
    2 cups thinly sliced zucchini
    ¾ cup chopped green pepper
    ¼ cup thinly sliced green onions
    1 cup (8-ounce container) plain yogurt
    1 teaspoon dill weed
    ¾ teaspoon salt
    ¼ teaspoon pepper
    2 tomatoes, cut into wedges

Cook orzo according to package directions; drain. Cool. (Rinse with cold water to cool quickly; drain well.) Combine drained orzo, zucchini, green pepper, and green onions in large bowl. Combine yogurt, dill weed, salt, and pepper in small bowl; blend well. Pour yogurt dressing over macaroni mixture; toss lightly. Chill. Just before serving add tomato wedges; toss lightly.

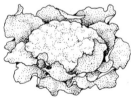

Tomato-Zucchini Orzo Salad; Tangy Ditalini Salad. Hershey Pasta Group

California Coleslaw

Makes about 8 cups
  1 medium head cabbage, shredded
  4 medium carrots, grated
  1 medium green pepper, chopped
  2 cups Lipton California Dip (see index)
  4 teaspoons vinegar

In large bowl, mix cabbage, carrots, and green pepper. Stir in Lipton California Dip blended with vinegar; chill.

Scandinavian Cucumber Salad

Makes about 4 servings
  ½ cup Lipton California Dip (see index)
  1 tablespoon vinegar
  1 teaspoon sugar
  ½ teaspoon salt
  ¼ teaspoon dill weed
  2 large cucumbers, thinly sliced

In medium bowl, combine all ingredients; chill.
Variation
Substitute raw cauliflowerets for the cucumbers.

Greek Salad

Makes 8 servings
  1½ quarts torn salad greens, washed and drained
  2 cucumbers, peeled and sliced
  6 scallions, chopped
    Salt and pepper to taste
    Olive oil
    Lemon juice
  8 small radishes, cleaned
  3 tomatoes, quartered
  16 anchovy fillets
  16 pitted ripe olives
  ½ pound feta cheese, crumbled

Place salad greens in a bowl and mix in cucumbers and scallions. Season. Dress with combined oil and lemon juice in proportions to suit your taste, using just enough to coat greens nicely. Arrange remaining ingredients attractively on top. Just before serving, toss to incorporate all ingredients.

Squash Salad

Makes 8 servings
  8 medium-size zucchini
  1 clove garlic
  ½ teaspoon cider vinegar
  1 small onion, minced
  3 stalks celery, chopped
  5 tablespoons French Dressing (see index)
    Salt and freshly ground pepper to taste
    Lettuce leaves
    Mayonnaise

Cut squash into pieces about ½ inch thick and place in a saucepan with a small amount of salted water, garlic, and vinegar. Cover and cook about 6 minutes, or until tender but not too soft. Drain; remove garlic. Chill zucchini. Add all other ingredients except the lettuce leaves and mayonnaise. Toss. Serve on lettuce leaves with mayonnaise on top.

Marinated Tomatoes

Makes 4 servings
  1 pound (about 3 medium) tomatoes, sliced
  ¼ pound part-skim milk mozzarella cheese, thinly sliced (optional)
  ⅓ cup Mazola Corn Oil
  3 tablespoons red wine vinegar
  3 tablespoons chopped parsley
  3 tablespoons finely chopped onion
  1 tablespoon finely chopped basil leaves or ½ teaspoon dried basil leaves
  ¼ teaspoon salt
  ¹⁄₁₆ teaspoon pepper

Arrange tomatoes and cheese in bottom of shallow dish. In small jar, with tight-fitting lid, place corn oil, vinegar, parsley, onion, basil, salt, and pepper. Cover; shake well. Pour over tomatoes and cheese. Cover; refrigerate several hours, spooning herb mixture over tomatoes occasionally.

Tomato Soup Salad

Makes 6 to 8 servings
  3 envelopes unflavored gelatin
  2½ cups water
  2 cans (10¾ ounces each) Campbell's Condensed Tomato Soup
  1 package (8 ounces) cream cheese
  2 tablespoons light cream
  ½ cup sliced stuffed olives
    Lettuce leaves
    Mayonnaise
    Finely chopped parsley

Soak gelatin in ¾ cup of the water 5 minutes. Stir over low heat until gelatin is dissolved. Stir gelatin and remaining water gradually into tomato soup. Pour half of the mixture into a lightly oiled 9-inch square pan. Chill until firm. Mash cream cheese until soft. Beat in cream. Fold in olives. Spread mixture evenly and carefully over firm gelatin. Pour remaining tomato mixture over cheese. Chill until firm. Cut into serving-size pieces, using a sharp knife. Loosen edges and remove pieces with a pancake turner. Serve salad on lettuce leaves with mayonnaise, garnished with finely chopped parsley.

Let's Hear It for Slaw

You make coleslaw of shredded cabbage—right? Right. But if you make it only of cabbage, you're missing a whole array of great-flavor salads. All sorts of vegetables lend themselves admirably to the slaw treatment, singly or in combinations that make for good looks as well as good taste. Try daikon, the huge, mild-flavored white Japanese radish. Or jícama, the big brown Mexican tuber with the unwiltable crispiness. Or white turnips, or golden rutabagas. Or firm red domestic radishes. Or pale green zucchini. Or sweet white parsnips. Or orange-bright carrots. Each of these has a delicious, distinctive flavor, generally quite different in the raw state from the taste of the same vegetable when cooked. Dress the vegetables simply, or zip them up with some finely chopped onion or a little pressed garlic, some snipped parsley or cilantro, some slivers of green or red or yellow sweet pepper (or all three). For a very delicate slaw, shred iceberg lettuce, toss with salt, pepper, and a little oil-rice vinegar-sugar-cream dressing. Seven different slaws 7 days in a row is no great challenge when you push your thoughts beyond cabbage.

Marinated Tomato Salad

Makes about 4 cups

  2 medium tomatoes, cut in wedges (2 cups)
  1 small zucchini, thinly sliced (1 cup)
  1 small yellow squash, thinly sliced (1 cup)
  1 small onion, thinly sliced (⅓ cup)
  ⅔ cup Mazola Corn Oil
  ⅓ cup white wine vinegar
  1 tablespoon chopped fresh mint or 1 teaspoon dried mint flakes
  1 teaspoon sugar (optional)

In large shallow dish, toss together tomatoes, zucchini, squash, and onion. In small bowl, stir together corn oil, vinegar, mint, and sugar. Pour over vegetables; toss to coat well. Cover; refrigerate several hours, stirring occasionally.

Celery Remoulade

Makes 4 servings

  2 bunches celery hearts
  2 tablespoons lemon juice
  2 teaspoons salt
  ¼ cup Grey Poupon Mustard
  ⅓ cup olive oil
  2 to 3 tablespoons white wine vinegar
  ½ teaspoon salt
  ½ teaspoon white pepper
    Salad greens
  3 tablespoons finely snipped parsley
  2 teaspoons finely snipped chives

Wash and dry celery. Cut into small julienne strips. Place in a bowl, add lemon juice and 2 teaspoons salt. Mix well and let stand at room temperature 1 hour. To make dressing, warm large electric mixer bowl by rinsing with hot water; dry. Place mustard in bowl. Beating at low-medium speed, add 3 tablespoons boiling water, a few drops at a time. Continuing to beat, add the oil, a few drops at a time. Add 2 tablespoons vinegar, ½ teaspoon salt, and the pepper. Taste and add more vinegar and seasoning, if necessary. Add dressing to celery and mix gently. Refrigerate covered overnight. Line a serving bowl with greens and mound celery in bowl. Sprinkle with parsley and chives.

Super Onion Salad

Makes 4 to 6 servings

  1 medium head broccoli, cut in florets
  1 medium-size red onion, thinly sliced
  1 cup cherry tomatoes, cut in halves
    Savory Vinaigrette Dressing (recipe follows)
  4 ounces (⅔ cup) feta cheese, diced
  ½ cup broken walnuts
    Lettuce

Steam broccoli 3 minutes. Drain. Cool to room temperature. Combine broccoli, onion, tomatoes, and ⅔ cup Savory Vinaigrette Dressing. Cover. Refrigerate 3 to 4 hours, stirring occasionally. Before serving, add cheese and walnuts; mix well. Serve on lettuce.

Savory Vinaigrette Dressing

Makes 1 cup

  ¾ cup vegetable oil
  ¼ cup white wine vinegar
  1 tablespoon prepared mustard
  2 cloves garlic, finely minced
  ¾ teaspoon dried leaf thyme, crumbled
  ½ teaspoon dried leaf oregano, crumbled
  ½ teaspoon salt
  ¼ teaspoon dried leaf basil, crumbled
  ⅛ teaspoon pepper

Combine all ingredients; mix well.

Centering on Vegetables

Main dishes that are not for vegetarians only, to celebrate the goodness, the healthiness, the variety of the vegetable kingdom.

Variable Vegetable Strata

Makes 4 servings

- 6 slices day-old bread
- 1 to 2 cups chopped cooked vegetables
- ½ cup (2 ounces) shredded cheddar cheese
- 6 eggs, lightly beaten
- 1 can (10¾ ounces) condensed cream of chicken soup, undiluted
- ½ cup milk
- 1 teaspoon prepared mustard
- ¼ to ½ teaspoon basil leaves, crushed
- ⅛ teaspoon pepper

Cut bread into ½-inch cubes. Sprinkle half the cubes into greased 8-inch square (or 2-quart rectangular) baking dish. Sprinkle vegetables and cheese over cubes. Top with remaining cubes.

Blend together eggs, soup, milk, and seasonings. Pour egg mixture over bread-vegetable mixture. Cover. Refrigerate several hours or overnight. Bake in a preheated 350°F. oven until golden brown, about 50 minutes.

Spring Vegetables

Makes 6 servings

- ½ pound tiny white onions, peeled
- 2 tablespoons butter or margarine
- 1 pound small new potatoes, scrubbed
- 6 carrots, peeled and cut into 1-inch pieces
- ½ cup chicken broth
- 2 tablespoons chopped fresh dill or 1 teaspoon dried dill
- ¾ teaspoon salt
- 1 cup peas (preferably fresh)

Sauté onions in butter until slightly browned, about 5 minutes. Add potatoes, carrots, chicken broth, dill and salt. Heat to boiling. Reduce heat and simmer covered 15 minutes. Add peas, re-cover, and cook 5 minutes longer, or until vegetables are just tender.

This recipe was provided by the makers of Saran Wrap™ brand plastic film.

Baked Vegetable Macedoine

Makes 8 to 10 servings

- 1 package (10 ounces) frozen mixed vegetables, thawed
- 1 package (10 ounces) frozen cauliflower, thawed
- 1 yellow squash, thinly sliced
- 1 zucchini squash, thinly sliced
- 1 potato, peeled and diced
- 1 cup cherry tomatoes, halved
- ½ cup chopped red onion
- 1 cup water
- ¼ cup oil
- 2 tablespoons Lea & Perrins Worcestershire Sauce
- 1 beef bouillon cube
- 2 large cloves garlic, crushed
- ½ teaspoon Italian seasoning

Place all vegetables in an ungreased 11x7x1½-inch baking pan. Toss gently; set aside. In a small saucepan, combine remaining ingredients. Bring to a boil; stir to dissolve bouillon cube. Pour over vegetables. Cover tightly. Bake in a preheated moderate oven (350°F.) until vegetables are crisp-tender, about 1 hour, stirring once.

> **Q.** *Why does cauliflower turn gray? Am I cooking it too long? It seems to be about the right texture when I cook it.*
> **A.** Are you using an aluminum pan? Cauliflower can turn gray when cooked in aluminum. Switch to a stainless steel or enamel-coated one. Be sure, when you buy cauliflower, that it is nice and white, and that the curd—the white part—is hard. Cook only until tender-crisp, in a proportion of ⅓ milk to ⅔ water for snowy whiteness.

Variable Vegetable Strata. American Egg Board

Garnishing Vegetables

When vegetables are used as a border around the main dish, they become an excellent garnish in themselves. But when they arrive at the table alone in a serving dish, they need a bit of dressing up—usually the addition of something that not only makes them look better, but taste better as well. Children know a fact that the rest of us try not to face: Vegetables can be dull. Good for you, but on the blah side. It's the garnish that takes them out of that class for youngsters and adults alike.

There is, however, no point in garnishing a vegetable that has lived and suffered too long. Old, tired vegetables are a waste of time and money. Young, tender fresh vegetables, or well-packaged frozen ones, are still a waste of time and money if they are overcooked, so that they come to the table limp and tasteless and mud colored.

The starting point for a vegetable that is welcomed is the cooking pot. If you have the oven on for some other purpose, baking vegetables (covered, without water, with butter if you wish and any other seasonings you like) is a great idea. They'll take longer than they would on top of the stove, but you'll be rewarded with better looks and better flavor. If you cook on top of the stove, follow two precepts: Be parsimonious with the water and brief with the cooking time. A good, heavy pan with a well-fitting lid can cook vegetables in a short time in virtualy no water. (Nor does it always have to be water—either broth or bouillon makes a fine vegetable-cookery medium.) Or pan the vegetables in a heavy, covered skillet that gives them plenty of room; use butter or margarine, a small amount of liquid, and seasonings as you wish. Using this method, cooking is even briefer. Coarsely shredded cabbage, sliced zucchini, and summer squash are three of the many vegetables that take kindly to panning. Spinach, to be at its best, needs only wilting in the water that clings to its leaves after washing. Other greens need a little longer—but not necessarily forever, with a ham hock, for heaven's sake!

For most vegetables, tender-crisp is the watchword. If your mother was one of those otherwise exemplary ladies who cooked vegetables until they screamed for mercy, you may find that the tender-crisp idea takes a bit of getting used to. But once over that hurdle, you'll love it. You'll realize you never really tasted vegetables before.

Fish Rolls with Vegetables and Clam Sauce

Makes 4 servings

       Water
  1 to 1½ pounds fish fillets
  ½ cup thinly sliced zucchini
  ½ cup thinly sliced carrots
  ½ cup onion rings
       Hot cooked noodles (optional)
  1 can (10½ ounces) white clam spaghetti sauce
  ½ cup diced tomato

In a large skillet, bring ½ inch water to a boil. Roll each fish fillet from the narrow end. Place in skillet along with zucchini, carrot, and onion. Simmer covered until fish is opaque and vegetables are tender, about 5 minutes. Place fish and vegetables on a serving platter over a bed of noodles, if desired; cover to keep warm. Drain and discard water from skillet. Add clam sauce and tomato. Simmer uncovered until tomato is softened, about 1 minute. Spoon over fish.

Italian Beef Stew

Makes 8 servings

  3 tablespoons olive oil
  3 pounds beef shoulder, cut into 2-inch cubes
  1 cup chopped onions
  ¼ pound sliced cooked ham, slivered
  1 clove garlic, minced
  1 can (28 ounces) recipe-ready crushed tomatoes
  2 tablespoons wine vinegar
  2 teaspoons basil leaves, crumbled
  2 teaspoons salt
  ¼ teaspoon ground black pepper
  1 can (14 ounces) artichoke hearts in brine, drained
  1 package (10 ounces) frozen peas, thawed
       Hot cooked fettuccine (optional)

In a large heavy ovenproof saucepan or a Dutch oven, heat oil until hot. Add beef a few pieces at a time; brown on all sides. Remove beef from saucepan; set aside. To saucepan, add onions, ham, and garlic; sauté over moderate heat for 2 minutes. Add tomatoes, vinegar, basil, salt, and black pepper; mix well. Return beef to pan. Cover and bake in a preheated slow oven (325°F.) until beef is fork-tender, about 2½ hours. Strain off fat. Add artichoke hearts and peas. Cover and bake 15 minutes longer. Serve with fettuccine noodles, if desired.

Broiled Steak Kebabs

Makes 6 servings
- ½ cup Mazola Corn Oil
- ⅓ cup red wine vinegar
- ¼ cup chopped onion
- 1 clove garlic, minced
- ½ teaspoon dried thyme leaves
- ½ teaspoon salt
- ¼ teaspoon pepper
- 1 1½- to 2-pound flank steak, cut in cubes or strips
  Assorted vegetables, such as sweet red pepper pieces and artichoke hearts, or cherry tomatoes and green pepper pieces, or zucchini slices and small whole cooked onions

In small bowl, stir together corn oil, vinegar, onion, garlic, thyme, salt, and pepper. Place flank steak pieces in shallow dish; pour marinade over steak. Cover; refrigerate 4 hours or overnight. Remove steak from marinade. Thread steak onto skewers alternately with assorted vegetables. Place kebabs on rack in broiler pan. Broil 4 to 5 inches from source of heat about 8 minutes, turning once and brushing with marinade, or until cooked to desired doneness.

Pasta Primavera

Makes 4 servings
- 3 tablespoons Mazola Corn Oil
- ¼ pound mushrooms, sliced
- 1 medium onion, cut in thin wedges
- 1 clove garlic, minced or pressed
- ½ pound broccoli, cut in flowerets, stalks sliced
- 2 medium carrots, cut in matchsticks
- 1 medium zucchini, thinly sliced
- ½ cup chopped parsley
- ½ cup chicken bouillon or vegetable broth
- 3 tablespoons lemon juice
- 1½ teaspoons dried basil leaves
- ¼ teaspoon pepper
- ½ pound Mueller's Spaghetti, cooked, drained
- ¼ cup chopped nuts
- 2 tablespoons grated Parmesan cheese

In large skillet, heat corn oil over medium-high heat. Add mushrooms, onion, and garlic. Stirring frequently, cook 1 minute. Add broccoli and carrots; cook 2 minutes longer. Stir in zucchini, parsley, chicken bouillon, lemon juice, basil, and pepper. Simmer 3 minutes. Place spaghetti on large platter or in bowl; top with sauce. Sprinkle with nuts and cheese.

Tender-Crisp Green Beans and Mushrooms

Makes 6 servings
- 1 pound green beans, cut in 2-inch pieces (4 cups)
- 1 tablespoon Mazola Corn Oil
- ½ pound mushrooms, sliced
- ¼ cup sliced green onion
- ½ teaspoon salt
  Dash pepper

Wash and drain beans but do not dry. In 12-inch skillet with tight-fitting lid, place corn oil, green beans, mushrooms, green onion, salt, and pepper. Cover and cook over medium heat 15 to 20 minutes, shaking skillet occasionally to prevent sticking.

Stir-Fry Chicken

Makes 4 servings
- 1 teaspoon Argo or Kingsford's Corn Starch
- ½ teaspoon salt
- ¼ teaspoon dried thyme leaves
- ¼ cup lemon juice
- ¼ cup water
- 3 tablespoons Mazola Corn Oil, divided
- 2 whole chicken breasts, boned, skinned, and cut into strips
- 1 large carrot, cut in 2-inch strips
- 1 pound zucchini, sliced (about 2 cups)
- 1 cup sliced celery
- 1 clove garlic, minced or pressed
- 1 teaspoon grated lemon rind

In small bowl, stir together cornstarch, salt, and thyme. Gradually stir in lemon juice and water until smooth. In wok or large skillet, heat 2 tablespoons of the corn oil over medium-high heat. Add chicken, one-half at a time; stir-fry 3 to 4 minutes, or until lightly browned. Remove from wok. Add remaining 1 tablespoon corn oil. Add carrots; stir-fry 1 to 2 minutes. Add zucchini; stir-fry 1 minute. Add celery, garlic, and lemon rind; stir-fry 1 minute. Return chicken to wok. Restir cornstarch mixture; stir into wok. Stirring constantly, bring to boil over medium heat and boil 1 minute.

Vegetable Medley. Argo/Kingsford's Corn Starch

Vegetable Medley

Makes 6 servings

6 **carrots, halved, cut in lengthwise strips (about 2 cups)**

3 **small zucchini, cut in ¼-inch diagonal slices (about 2 cups)**

½ **pint cherry tomatoes (about 10) or 1 package (10 ounces) frozen peas, thawed**

1 **cup herb-seasoned croutons**

2 **tablespoons Argo or Kingsford's Corn Starch**

1 **teaspoon salt**

¼ **teaspoon pepper**

1½ **cups milk**

1 **teaspoon dried basil leaves**

Cook carrots in boiling salted water about 5 minutes, or until tender-crisp; drain. In shallow 1-quart baking dish, toss together carrots, zucchini, tomatoes, and croutons. In 2-quart saucepan, stir together cornstarch, salt, and pepper. Gradually stir in milk until smooth. Add margarine. Stirring constantly, bring to boil over medium heat and boil 1 minute. Pour over vegetables. Sprinkle with basil. Bake in 350°F. oven 25 minutes, or until vegetables are tender.

Ratatouille Crêpes

Makes 7 to 8 servings
   3 **zucchini, sliced**
   2 **crookneck squash, sliced**
  10 **mushrooms, sliced**
   1 **onion, sliced**
   1 **green pepper, cut in strips**
   1 **clove garlic, minced**
   3 **tablespoons pure vegetable oil**
   1 **can (6 ounces) Hunt's Tomato Paste**
     Water
   2 **tablespoons chopped pimientos**
   1 **teaspoon salt**
   1 **teaspoon Italian herb seasoning**
   ¼ **teaspoon pepper**
  14 **to 16 Crêpes (recipe follows)**
     Chopped parsley

In a skillet, sauté zucchini, crookneck, mushrooms, onion, green pepper, and garlic in oil until vegetables are limp. Stir in Hunt's Tomato Paste, 1 can water, pimiento, salt, Italian herb seasoning, and pepper. Simmer 10 to 15 minutes. Place about 3 tablespoons of vegetable mixture down center of each crêpe; fold sides to overlap. Place on serving plates, allowing 2 per serving. Spoon remaining mixture over folded crêpes. Top with chopped parsley.

Crêpes

Makes 14 to 16 crêpes
   ⅔ **cup milk**
   ⅔ **cup water**
   2 **eggs**
   1 **egg yolk**
  1¼ **cups sifted all-purpose flour**
   ¼ **teaspoon salt**
   5 **tablespoons melted butter, divided**

In a blender container, combine milk, water, eggs, and egg yolk; add flour, salt, and 2 tablespoons melted butter; blend. Heat 8-inch crêpe pan over high heat. Remove pan from heat; brush lightly with melted butter. Pour in a scant 3 tablespoons batter, tilting pan to thinly coat bottom. Return to heat. When crêpe is lightly browned, turn and brown other side.

Ratatouille Crêpes. Photograph was provided by Hunt-Wesson Foods, Inc.; photography by Tom Kelley Studios

Asparagus Roll-Ups

Makes 3 servings
  1 package (10 ounces) frozen asparagus spears
  1 can (7 ounces) SPAM®, diced
  ¼ cup Swiss Cheese Sauce (recipe follows)
 12 slices soft white bread
  2 tablespoons butter or margarine

Cook asparagus according to package directions; drain. Cut asparagus crosswise in ½-inch pieces. Combine asparagus, SPAM®, and Swiss Cheese Sauce. Remove crusts from bread; flatten by rolling with a rolling pin. Spread butter lightly on one side of each bread slice. Mound some SPAM® mixture along one edge of unbuttered side of each bread slice; roll up. Place close together in baking dish, seam side down. Bake in 425°F. oven 15 minutes, or until rolls are lightly browned. Serve with additional Swiss Cheese Sauce.

Swiss Cheese Sauce

  1 tablespoon butter or margarine
  1 tablespoon all-purpose flour
  ¼ teaspoon salt
  ⅛ teaspoon paprika
    Ground nutmeg to taste
    Pepper to taste
  1 cup milk
  1 cup shredded Swiss cheese

In small saucepan, melt butter; blend in flour, salt, paprika, nutmeg, and pepper. Mix in milk; cook over medium heat, stirring until mixture thickens and boils. Add cheese; stir until melted.
Nice to know: You'll have about 1¾ cups of sauce left over. Refrigerate and reheat for use another day.

Beef à la Reine

Makes 5 to 6 servings
  1 jar (2½ ounces) Armour Star Sliced Dried
      Beef, cut in strips
  2 cups sliced mushrooms
  2 tablespoons finely chopped onion
  ¼ cup butter or margarine
  ¼ cup all-purpose flour
 1¼ cups milk
  1 cup sour cream
  1 cup (4 ounces) shredded cheddar cheese
    Hot cooked asparagus spears

In fry pan, cook dried beef, mushrooms, and onion in butter on medium heat 5 minutes; blend in flour. Gradually add milk; cook, stirring until thickened. Stir in sour cream; sprinkle with cheese. Cover pan; allow to cook over low heat 5 minutes, or until cheese melts. Stir lightly. Serve over asparagus.

Plantation Blackeyes

Makes 6 to 8 servings
  1 pound dry blackeyes
  ¼ pound bacon
  1 cup chopped onions
  2 cups canned whole tomatoes
 1½ cups water
  2 teaspoons salt
  ¼ teaspoon pepper
  ¾ teaspoon oregano
  ½ teaspoon thyme
  ½ teaspoon rosemary
 1½ cups grated cheddar cheese

Wash, sort, and soak blackeyes. Cut bacon into 1-inch pieces. Cook in Dutch oven or heavy pot until fat is rendered. Add onions and cook until tender. Add tomatoes with their liquid, breaking them up with a spoon. Add water, seasonings, and soaked drained blackeyes. Simmer covered until beans are just tender (about 30 minutes). Stir in cheese, pour mixture into a 3-quart rectangular casserole, and bake uncovered 30 to 40 minutes at 375°F.

Sweet and Sour Cabbage Rolls

Makes 4 to 5 servings
  8 to 10 large cabbage leaves
  1 pound lean ground beef
  ½ cup Sun-Maid® Seedless Raisins, divided
  ⅓ cup long-grained rice
  3 tablespoons minced onion
  2 tablespoons chopped parsley
  1 tablespoon lemon juice
 1½ teaspoons basil
  1 teaspoon salt
  ¼ teaspoon freshly ground pepper
  ¼ teaspoon paprika
  1 can (16 ounces) stewed tomatoes
  1 can (10½ ounces) condensed beef broth,
      undiluted
    Sour cream

Blanch the cabbage leaves in boiling salted water for 3 to 5 minutes; drain and set aside. Combine the meat with ¼ cup of the raisins and the rice, onion, parsley, lemon juice, basil, salt, pepper, paprika, and ½ cup water. Mix well. Place a portion of the meat mixture in the center of each cabbage leaf. Fold in sides and roll from stem end. Place, seam side down, in a large skillet. Add the remaining ¼ cup raisins and the tomatoes and beef broth; bring to a boil. Reduce heat and simmer covered 50 minutes. Serve in bowls, spooning the raisin sauce over the cabbage rolls and topping with dollops of sour cream.

Unusual Vegetables

The *boniato,* also called the Cuban sweet potato or the white sweet potato, is a tuber much liked in Central America; its flesh is white, but sweeter than ordinary white potatoes, and drier in texture than the sweet potato. Cook and serve in any way you would a sweet potato. *Celeriac* is also known as celery root and knob celery; looking old before its time with its irregular shape, blemished brown skin, and thin, hairy roots, it must be peeled before eating. Then it displays pale crisp flesh that can be eaten either raw or cooked. Raw, its most familiar use is as céleri rémoulade—julienne strips of the raw vegetable topped with a mayonnaise-based sauce. Cooked, it can be served as a simple vegetable with butter or a cream sauce, or added to soups and stews. Familiar in Europe for a long time, celeriac is finding some followers here, and is available in many supermarkets. *Chayote* is a cousin of squash and cucumber and has been a longtime favorite in Mexico and Central America. The vegetable is shaped like a plump pear; its pale green skin is tender enough to eat when the chayote is young, but some prefer to peel it when it is older. The flesh, a still-paler green, is tender—it cooks in a very brief time—and mild in flavor. Available in many supermarkets, try it boiled and buttered, mashed, or dipped in batter and deep-fried. The *Jerusalem artichoke* suffers from an identity crisis—because it has nothing to do with Jerusalem and is not a relative of the more-familiar globe artichoke, growers and distributors keep trying to change its name. "Sunroot" and "sunchoke" are two of the names favored, because the tuber is the root of a species of sunflower. Eaten raw, the vegetable has a crunchy texture and a winning flavor; cooked (in any manner you would cook a potato) its texture is like that of a cooked chestnut and its flavor reminiscent of a globe artichoke. Available in supermarkets. *Kaboche* is a handsome variety of squash, deep green outside, richly golden inside, and shaped like a small pumpkin —in fact, it is sometimes called the Japanese pumpkin-squash. Bake, boil, or fry it, as you would winter squash, or use in custards and pies, like pumpkin, which it resembles in flavor. Available in some supermarkets. *Kale* is an ancestor of the cabbage, used in Europe—especially Scotland—since prehistoric times. Its ruffled green leaves grow off a central stalk, not forming a head as cabbage does. Prepare as you would spinach, but it will require a slightly longer cooking time. *Scorzonera* is a tuber, also called black salsify, and is a member of the same oyster-plant family, so-called because its flavor resembles oysters. Prepare as you would any root vegetable; it can be fried, baked, boiled, or sautéed. *Sugar snap peas* are a recent "invention," a cross between the Chinese snow pea and the conventional garden pea with which we are so familiar, and offering the best of both. Like snow peas, the pod is deliciously edible. Like conventional peas, the pod is filled with plump little green globes. Eat raw in salads, with a dip, or split and stuffed with a savory mixture as an hors d'oeuvre; or cook them briefly, sautéed or steamed, or in stir-fry dishes. Find them in the spring in supermarkets, but be sharp-eyed—no great quantity is produced as yet, but more are grown every year. *Sweet onions* are known as Maui (from Hawaii) or Vidalia (from Georgia), but they are beginning to be grown in many other places. Yes, all onions are somewhat sweet, but these are so sweet and so mild that you can, if you've a mind to, eat them out of hand as you would an apple. Wonderful in salads and in onion sandwiches or served with a dip. Or cook briefly and serve buttered or creamed. Available in upscale greengrocers, or by mail—look for ads in the food-and-cooking magazines. *Yellow Finnish potatoes* are not from Finland, but from the state of Washington. They are very moist, with a naturally buttery texture and flavor. Definitely the aristocrat of the potato family, they are more expensive than the common varieties, largely because present crops are small; but as the potato catches on—and it surely will—more will be available. Cook and serve as you would any potato.

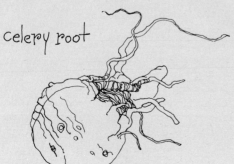

celery root

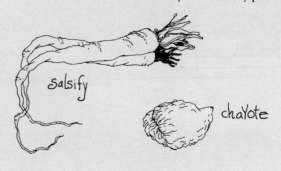

salsify

chayote

Eggplant à la Smyrna

Makes 4 servings

    1 ¾-pound eggplant
    4 tablespoons olive oil
    1 medium-size onion, sliced
    ¼ cup water
    ½ cup tomato sauce
      Pinch sugar
    ¾ teaspoon salt
      Pepper
      Parboiled or leftover meat (optional)

Peel and slice eggplant lengthwise about ½ inch thick. Soak the eggplant in cold salted water for 5 to 10 minutes to extract bitterness. Braise in hot olive oil and transfer to saucepan or shallow casserole, draining off all but 1 tablespoon olive oil. Use more olive oil if necessary, but be sure to leave only 1 tablespoon of oil after draining. Add ¼ cup water, onion, tomato sauce, and sugar. Season and simmer in covered pan until the eggplant is soft. Parboiled or leftover meat may be added 20 minutes after the ingredients are put in casserole. Continue to cook for 15 to 20 minutes. Serve hot.

Baked Eggplant Italiano

Makes 4 servings

    1 eggplant (about 1¼ pounds)
      Salt
      All-purpose flour
    2 eggs, well beaten
      Cooking oil
    1½ cups (6 ounces) shredded mozzarella cheese,
        divided
    1 can (7 ounces) SPAM®, diced
    1 cup Marinara Sauce (recipe follows)

Cut unpeeled eggplant lengthwise in ¼-inch slices. Lightly salt and place on plate; place a baking pan filled with heavy cans on top of eggplant. Let stand 1 hour; drain off accumulated liquid. Dip each slice in flour, then into beaten eggs. Sauté in oil in large skillet, a few slices at a time, until browned on both sides. Drain on paper towel. Reserve about ⅓ cup mozzarella cheese; combine remaining cheese with SPAM®. Spread about 2 tablespoons sauce over bottom of lightly greased 1-quart baking dish. Cover with a layer of eggplant. Add layer of SPAM® mixture; spread with sauce. Repeat layers ending with sauce. Sprinkle with reserved cheese. Bake in 400°F. oven 15 minutes, or until mixture is hot and cheese melts on top. Let stand 5 minutes before cutting.

Pasta Primavera (page 77); Marinated Tomatoes (page 72). Mazola Corn Oil

Beef à la Reine (page 80). Armour Food Company

Marinara Sauce

    ¼ cup chopped onion
    ¼ cup chopped celery
    1 clove garlic, minced
    1 tablespoon pure vegetable oil
    1 can (15 ounces) tomato sauce
    2 tablespoons red wine
    ¼ teaspoon basil
    ¼ teaspoon oregano
    ¼ teaspoon salt
    ⅛ teaspoon pepper
    1 bay leaf

In a medium saucepan, sauté onion, celery, and garlic in oil. Add remaining ingredients and simmer 15 minutes.

Nice to know: You'll have an extra cup of sauce. Freeze it to use another day.

Baked Eggplant with Cheese

Makes 8 servings

- ¼ cup fine dry bread crumbs
- ½ cup sifted all-purpose flour
- 1 teaspoon salt
- 2 medium-size eggplants, peeled and sliced
- 1 cup milk
- ½ cup butter, divided
- 2 eggs, beaten
- ¾ pound mozzarella cheese, grated
- 3 tablespoons grated Parmesan cheese

Combine bread crumbs, flour, and salt on a piece of waxed paper or in a wide, shallow dish. Dip eggplant slices in milk, then in crumb mixture, coating well. Melt half the butter in a skillet. Sauté the eggplant until browned on both sides, adding more butter if necessary. Combine eggs with the two cheeses. Arrange half the eggplant on the bottom of a 13x9x2-inch baking dish. Spread cheese mixture over it; top with remaining eggplant. Bake in a preheated 375°F. oven for 20 minutes.

Helpful to know: Prepare this the day before, if you like, and refrigerate. In that case, bake 30 minutes.

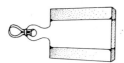

Athenian Stuffed Eggplant

Makes 4 servings

- 2 eggplants (1 pound each)
- 1 medium-size onion, chopped
- ¼ cup olive oil
- ¼ pound mushrooms, sliced
- 2 medium-size tomatoes, chopped
- ½ cup Sun-Maid® Zante Currants
- 1½ teaspoons salt
- 1½ teaspoons oregano, crumbled
- ¾ cup macaroni, cooked
- 2 cups shredded Monterey Jack cheese, divided

Cut the eggplant in half lengthwise and remove the pulp with a paring knife and spoon, leaving a ¼-inch shell; coarsely chop the pulp. In a large skillet, sauté the onion in oil until soft but not browned; add the chopped eggplant and cook 3 minutes longer. Preheat the oven to 375°F. Stir in the mushrooms, tomatoes, currants, salt, and oregano. Cover and simmer for 5 minutes; remove from heat and stir in the macaroni and 1 cup of the cheese. Spoon into the eggplant shells and sprinkle with the remaining 1 cup cheese. Bake for 20 minutes.

How to Prepare Eggplant

Eggplant can be peeled or not as you choose. Unless the skin is unusually tough, leave it in place—it has excellent flavor, and helps hold the eggplant together in the finished dish.

However you prepare it, eggplant cooks in a short time. Boiling (cubes, 6 to 7 minutes) is the least desirable method; it leaches out most of the flavor. It may be sliced and pan-fried in oil—preferably olive oil, as the two flavors have an affinity for one another—either plain or breaded (5 to 8 minutes, depending on thickness of slices), but it absorbs a lot of oil in the process. If you want plain sliced eggplant as a vegetable, brush the slices on both sides with oil or soft butter and broil (5 to 10 minutes per side) until brown. It may also be deep-fried—again, plain or breaded. Or it may be baked whole (20 to 30 minutes) until tender, halved, the meat scooped out and combined with other ingredients, returned to the half shells and reheated in the oven.

Lamb and eggplant are the best of friends, and the flavors of that excellent combination are enhanced with onion, tomato, garlic, and mushrooms. Eggplant parmigiana—with not only Parmesan but also mozzarella, and a richly seasoned tomato sauce—is a classic Italian dish. Eggplant caviar—caponata—is another. Stuffed eggplant, particularly if the stuffing combines the eggplant pulp with rice and either ground lamb or pork sausage—particularly the anise-flavored Italian sweet sausage—is a gustatory triumph. Ratatouille, a superb hodgepodge of eggplant, onion, tomatoes, and zucchini or little yellow summer squash cooked in a garlicky olive oil, is delicious hot or cold.

Some eggplants are bitter. To avoid carrying this taste into the finished dish, slice the eggplant and place the slices on a flat surface in a single layer. Sprinkle liberally with salt; turn over and repeat. Cover with wax paper or foil and weight with a cookie sheet on which you have placed several heavy food cans. Let stand about 1 hour. Rinse the eggplant very well under cold running water, and pat dry with absorbent paper.

Eggplant is, of course, to eat. But it can also be for show. An attractive centerpiece—for, say, an autumn buffet—can be composed of sleek purple eggplants, green peppers, small yellow crookneck squash, and ears of colorful Indian corn, liberally heaped on a flat wooden tray or directly on a brightly colored tablecloth.

Savory Onion Casserole

Makes 6 servings

- 2 pounds (about 26) small white onions, peeled
- ¼ cup plus 3 tablespoons butter, divided
- ¼ cup all-purpose flour
- 2 cups milk
- 1 teaspoon Worcestershire sauce
- ¼ teaspoon salt
- ⅛ teaspoon pepper
- ¼ cup (2 ounces) crumbled blue cheese
- ⅔ cup packaged plain dry bread crumbs

In a large saucepan, bring 1 inch water to a boil; add onions and steam covered 10 minutes. Meanwhile, in medium saucepan melt ¼ cup butter; stir in flour. Cook 1 minute. Gradually add milk, Worcestershire, salt, and pepper; stir until mixture boils and thickens. Stir in cheese until melted. Drain onions; place in a 1½-quart casserole. Pour cheese sauce over onions; mix well. In a small skillet or saucepan, melt remaining 3 tablespoons butter; stir in bread crumbs. Sprinkle crumbs over casserole. Bake in 350°F. oven 20 minutes, until onions are tender and crumbs are lightly browned.

Onion-Mushroom Pie

Makes 6 servings

- Pastry for a 2-crust pie (see index)
- ¼ cup butter or margarine
- 3 large onions, sliced (3 cups)
- ½ pound fresh mushrooms, sliced (2 cups)
- 3 tablespoons cornstarch
- 1 cup cottage cheese
- ¼ cup chopped parsley
- 2 tablespoons dry sherry
- ¼ teaspoon salt
- ⅛ teaspoon pepper

Roll two-thirds of pastry dough into a 12-inch circle. Line a 9-inch pie plate with pastry. Roll remaining dough into a rectangle 5x9 inches. Cut out 10½-inch strips for lattice top. Set aside. In large skillet, melt butter; sauté onions and mushrooms until soft and golden. Stir in cornstarch. Add cottage cheese, parsley, sherry, salt, and pepper; mix well. Spoon mixture into prepared pie shell. Moisten edge of bottom crust with water. Weave strips of dough over filling to make a lattice top. Press strips to bottom crust. Fold crust over strips; form standing rim; flute. Bake in a 400°F. oven 40 minutes until pastry is golden and filling is bubbly. Cool 10 minutes before slicing.

Two-Crust 9-inch Pie

Makes one 9-inch pie

- 2 cups sifted Martha White All-Purpose Flour
- 1 teaspoon salt
- ⅔ cup vegetable shortening
- 4½ to 5 tablespoons cold water

Combine flour and salt in bowl. Cut in half of the shortening with pastry blender or 2 knives until mixture is consistency of coarse crumbs. Cut in remaining shortening until mixture is consistency of small peas. Sprinkle a small amount of water over mixture; stir with fork. Repeat with remaining water until dough is moist enough to form a ball but not sticky. Shape into ball. Divide dough in half. Flatten dough on floured board or pastry cloth. Roll gently with rolling pin outward from center to ⅛-inch thickness. Roll into circle about 1 inch larger than pie pan. Fold dough in half. Transfer to pie pan; unfold and fit loosely into pan without stretching dough. Use small ball of excess dough to press gently into bottom and sides of pan. If dough tears, patch by moistening with a little water and pressing torn edges together. Trim flush with rim of pie pan. Pour filling into crust. Moisten edge of bottom crust with water. Roll out remaining dough 1 inch larger than pan. Fold in half. Carefully place on top of filling; unfold. Press edges together, tucking top of pastry under edge of bottom pastry. Flute edges. Cut slits in top to allow steam to escape. Bake as directed.

Note: To flute edge, press knuckle of middle finger into inside edge of dough while pressing thumb and index fingers of other hand from other side. Repeat procedure to flute entire edge.

Potato Waffles

Makes 8 to 10 servings

- 1¼ cups sifted all-purpose flour
- ¼ cup instant mashed-potato granules
- 2 teaspoons sugar
- 2 teaspoons baking powder
- ½ teaspoon salt
- 3 eggs
- ⅓ cup salad oil
- 1½ cups milk

Sift together flour, potato granules, sugar, baking powder, and salt. Beat eggs thoroughly and add salad oil and milk. Combine liquid and dry ingredients and blend thoroughly. Preheat waffle iron and pour batter into center of lower half until it spreads to about 1 inch from edges. Bake until nicely browned.

Zucchini Mushroom Bake (page 89). Caloric Corporation

Scalloped Potato-Beer Casserole

Makes 8 servings

  4 **large baking potatoes**
  1 **cup thinly sliced onions**
1½ **teaspoons salt**
  1 **teaspoon garlic salt**
  2 **teaspoons sugar**
  1 **teaspoon paprika**
  2 **tablespoons all-purpose flour**
  4 **tablespoons butter**
 12 **ounces Lowenbrau beer**
 ¼ **pound grated Swiss cheese**

Broiled Steak Kebabs (page 77); Stir-Fry Chicken (page 77); Tender-Crisp Green Beans and Mushrooms (page 77). Mazola Corn Oil

Peel potatoes and slice ⅛ inch thick. Layer a buttered casserole dish with one-quarter of the potatoes. Spread evenly on bottom of dish. Sprinkle potatoes with one-quarter the amount of sliced onions. Combine in a small bowl the salt, garlic salt, sugar, paprika, and flour. Blend these ingredients well. Sprinkle 2½ teaspoons of dry mix evenly on top of the first layer. Dot with 1 tablespoon butter in pieces. Continue layering with this procedure for 3 more layers. Pour Lowenbrau over potato casserole and top with grated cheese. Bake in 350°F. oven for 1 hour.

Meaty Potatoes au Gratin

Makes 4 servings
   1 package (5½ounces) potatoes au gratin mix
   1 can (7 ounces) SPAM®, diced
   ¼ cup chopped green pepper
   2 cups boiling water
   ⅔ cup milk
   1 medium tomato

In 1½-quart casserole, combine potatoes, sauce mix, SPAM®, and green pepper. Pour in boiling water and milk; stir to mix well. Bake uncovered in 400°F. oven 25 minutes. Stir well. Slice tomato; halve each slice. Overlap tomato slices on top of casserole. Return to oven and bake 10 minutes longer. Let stand 5 minutes before serving.

Fresh Potato Mélange

Makes 4 to 6 servings
   ¼ cup butter or margarine
   2 large potatoes, pared and cut in julienne strips
      (about 3½ cups)
   1 large onion, chopped (1 cup)
   1 large carrot, thinly sliced (¾ cup)
   2 ribs celery, sliced (1 cup)
   1 clove garlic, chopped
   2 cups chicken broth
   1 bay leaf
   ¼ teaspoon dried leaf thyme, crumbled
   ¼ teaspoon salt
   ⅛ teaspoon pepper

In large skillet, melt butter; sauté potatoes, onion, carrot, celery, and garlic 2 to 3 minutes, stirring occasionally. Stir in broth, bay leaf, thyme, salt, and pepper. Bring to boiling, reduce heat, and simmer covered 10 minutes. Uncover, stir, and cook 5 minutes longer. With a slotted spoon, transfer vegetables to serving bowl; keep warm. Reduce cooking liquid over high heat until slightly thickened, about 2 minutes. Pour over vegetables.

Cheesy New Potato Casserole

Makes 6 to 8 servings
   1½ pounds new potatoes (18 small)
   ½ cup sliced scallions
   1 pound muenster (or mozzarella) cheese, sliced
      thinly
   4 large eggs
   ½ cup milk
   ½ teaspoon pepper
   ⅓ cup packaged seasoned dry bread crumbs

Scrub potatoes well. Steam in 1-inch boiling, salted water 20 to 25 minutes until tender; rinse with cold water; slice thinly. Butter a 7½x11½-inch baking dish. Arrange one-third of the potatoes in the dish; top with half the scallions and half the cheese. Repeat layers, ending with potatoes. In a small bowl, beat together eggs, milk, and pepper; pour over potatoes. Sprinkle top evenly with bread crumbs. Cover. Bake in 375°F. oven 25 minutes. Remove cover and bake 10 to 15 minutes longer until potatoes are tender.

Clam-Stuffed Potatoes

Makes 4 servings
   4 large Idaho® Potatoes
   1 can (6½ ounces) minced clams, drained, with
      ¼ cup liquid reserved
   2 tablespoons butter or margarine
   2 tablespoons finely chopped onion
   1 tablespoon packaged seasoned dry bread
      crumbs
   ¾ teaspoon dried leaf oregano
   ¼ teaspoon salt
   ¼ teaspoon pepper
   2 tablespoons grated Parmesan cheese

Scrub potatoes, dry, and prick with a fork. Bake in a 425°F. oven 55 to 65 minutes, until soft. Reduce oven temperature to 350°F. When potatoes are done, cut slice from top of each. Carefully scoop out potato without breaking skin. Set skins aside. In medium mixing bowl, whip potatoes. Add reserved liquid from clams, butter, onion, bread crumbs, oregano, salt and pepper; beat until smooth. Stir in minced clams. Spoon potato mixture into reserved potato skins and sprinkle with cheese. Bake in a 350°F. oven 20 to 30 minutes, until potatoes are heated through.

Potato Pancakes

Makes 8 to 10 pancakes
   2 eggs
   ½ small onion, cut up
   ¼ teaspoon baking powder
   1 teaspoon salt
   ¼ teaspoon all-purpose flour
   2½ cups cubed, pared potatoes

Put eggs, onion, baking powder, salt, flour, and 1 cup potatoes into blender container. Cover; blend at medium speed until potatoes are grated and ingredients are thoroughly combined. Add remaining potatoes. Cover; blend at medium speed several seconds or just until potatoes are grated. Pour small amounts onto heated, well-greased griddle or skillet. Fry until golden brown on both sides.

Latkes (Potato Pancakes with Matzo Meal)

Use only 1 egg and omit baking powder and flour in Potato Pancake recipe. Prepare recipe through processing of potatoes. Stir in 2 tablespoons matzo meal. Heat ½-inch depth of vegetable oil in skillet. Pour small amounts of batter into hot oil. Fry until golden brown on both sides. Drain on paper towels. Serve with fresh applesauce.

Spinach Pie

Makes 8 servings

  2 **pounds raw spinach**
  2 **teaspoons salt**
 ¼ **teaspoon pepper**
 ¾ **cup olive oil, divided**
  1 **cup chopped scallions**
  2 **tablespoons minced fresh dill weed**
  2 **tablespoons finely snipped parsley**
 ½ **pound feta (Greek) cheese, mashed**
 ¼ **teaspoon pepper**
10 **sheets phyllo pastry**

Wash the spinach, drain, and chop it. Sprinkle with the salt and ¼ teaspoon pepper. Let stand 1 hour. Drain thoroughly. Heat ¼ cup olive oil in a skillet; sauté the scallions 5 minutes. Mix in the spinach and cook over low heat 5 minutes, stirring frequently. Turn into a bowl; add dill, parsley, cheese, and remaining pepper. Brush an 8x12-inch baking pan with oil. Line with 1 sheet of pastry. Brush with oil and cover with 4 more sheets, brushing each with oil. Spread the spinach mixture over the pastry and cover with remaining 5 sheets, brushing each with oil. Score the top into squares and brush lightly with cold water. Bake in a preheated 350°F. oven for 40 minutes, or until browned. Cool 10 minutes; cut into squares.

Helpful to know: Buy phyllo pastry in Greek, Armenian or Turkish stores or in gourmet shops—or use packaged strudel leaves.

Zucchini-Mushroom Bake

Makes 4 to 6 servings

 3 **slices bacon, diced**
 2 **medium-size zucchini (1 pound), thinly sliced**
¼ **pound mushrooms, sliced**
 1 **large tomato, diced**
½ **teaspoon salt, or to taste**
¼ **teaspoon freshly ground pepper**
½ **teaspoon oregano**

Cook bacon on stove in ovenproof casserole until done. Remove bacon from casserole with slotted spoon; drain on paper towel. Stir zucchini, mushrooms, tomato, salt, pepper, and oregano into drippings in casserole. Cover; bake at 350°F. 25 to 35 minutes until vegetables are tender. Stir and sprinkle with crumbled bacon before serving.

Saucy Vegetables

Many good vegetables are better—and more acceptable to the vegetable-haters in the crowd—when they are served with a sauce. White sauce is good. Cheese sauce is better. Best of all is hollandaise—but the very mention of the word makes many home cooks fall into a cold-sweat panic. These, if they serve hollandasie at all, have recourse to the several canned brands, some of which taste more like can than hollandaise, or the envelopes of hollandaise sauce mix. Some of the latter make a reasonably acceptable sauce, but it's not hollandaise; others produce a glunk closely resembling the flour-and-water paste Grandma used to mix for the kids.

Listen carefully. Hollandaise is not all that difficult to produce, particularly if you use a blender. In a small saucepan, over low heat, melt ½ cup (1 stick) of butter. As it melts, place in the blender container 3 egg yolks, 1 to 2 tablespoons lemon juice, 2 drops hot pepper sauce. Cover blender and process a few seconds to blend the ingredients. Remove center cap from cover. As soon as the butter foams, remove it quickly from heat and pour into blender, turned to high, very slowly. Bingo! Lovely thick, golden hollandaise, ready to use.

You're still not convinced? Or you'd like to be able to make the sauce well in advance of dinner and hold it until you're ready to serve? Then try this excellent hollandaiselike sauce that even the klutziest cook can do nothing to ruin. Heat water in the bottom of a double boiler until it reaches the simmering point, just below boiling. Adjust heat to maintain this temperature. In the top of the double boiler, place 3 egg yolks; stir to break them up. Add 1 cup sour cream, 1 tablespoon (or more, if you like things very tart) lemon juice, ½ teaspoon salt, and 2 drops hot pepper sauce. Stir to mix well, and put the top of the double boiler in place over the bottom. Now you can ignore the sauce as long as you wish. Forget it, even for an hour or two. When ready to serve, stir thoroughly and ladle over asparagus, brussels sprouts, broccoli, braised leeks, or any vegetable you have in mind. Makes a great sauce for fish, as well.

What Goes with What?

Vegetable side dishes to accompany meats, poultry, and fish, or good enough—and substantial enough—to stand alone in their infinite tastiness.

Creamed Vegetables

Makes 6 to 8 servings

- 2 packages (10 ounces each) frozen mixed vegetables (or frozen cauliflower, asparagus, peas, broccoli, or spinach)
- 1 can (10¾ ounces) Campbell's Condensed Cheddar Cheese Soup
- ⅓ cup heavy cream

Cook vegetables according to package directions. Drain. Add soup and cream to vegetables. Simmer until bubbly. Serve hot.

Variation

If desired, creamed vegetables may be poured into a shallow 1-quart casserole and topped with ½ cup dry bread crumbs mixed with ¼ cup melted butter. Bake in a preheated 400°F. oven for 15 minutes, or until top is lightly browned.

Sweet 'n' Sour Stir-Fry

Makes about 6 servings

- 2 tablespoons oil
- 1 cup thinly sliced carrots
- 1 cup Chinese pea pods
- 1 small green pepper, cut into chunks
- 1 tomato, cut into wedges
- 1 cup sliced water chestnuts
- ½ cup sliced cucumber
- ¾ cup Wish-Bone® Sweet 'n Spicy French or Russian Dressing
- 2 tablespoons brown sugar
- 2 teaspoons soy sauce
  Sesame seed (optional)

In medium skillet, heat oil and cook carrots, pea pods, and green pepper until tender, about 5 minutes. Add tomato, water chestnuts, cucumber, and Wish-Bone Sweet 'n Spicy French Dressing blended with brown sugar and soy sauce. Simmer 5 minutes or until vegetables are crisp-tender. Top, if desired, with sesame seed.

Elegant Puffed Broccoli (page 96).
Hellmann's/Best Foods Real Mayonnaise

Indian Summer Vegetables

Makes 10 to 12 servings

- 2 ears fresh corn
- 3 tablespoons butter or margarine
- 2 medium-size green peppers, cut into strips
- 2 medium onions, sliced
- 6 medium zucchini, cut into ½-inch slices
- 4 medium tomatoes, quartered
- 1½ teaspoons salt
- ¼ teaspoon coarsely ground black pepper
- ¼ teaspoon sweet basil
- ½ cup grated Parmesan cheese

Cut corn off the cob. Preheat Sunbeam Multi-Cooker Frypan to 360°F. Add butter and melt. Add green peppers and onions. Cook covered 5 minutes, stirring once or twice. Add ¼ cup water and remaining ingredients except Parmesan. Cook covered 10 minutes, or until vegetables are crisp-tender, not mushy. Shake occasionally during cooking time. Serve sprinkled with grated cheese.

Bubble and Squeak

Makes 6 servings

- ¼ cup beef or bacon drippings
- ¼ cup chopped onion
- 2 cups sliced cooked potato
- 1 cup sliced cooked carrots
- 2 cups shredded cooked cabbage
- 2 tablespoons Lea & Perrins Worcestershire Sauce
  Salt

In a large heavy skillet, heat drippings. Add onion; sauté until tender, about 5 minutes. Add potato; sauté on both sides until browned. Stir in carrots and cabbage; stir-fry until vegetables are golden and "squeak" in the skillet. Stir in Lea & Perrins and salt to taste.

Spicy Vegetable Medley

Makes 6 servings
 1 medium-size onion, sliced
 2 tablespoons butter or margarine
 ⅓ cup Sun-Maid® Puffed Seeded Muscat Raisins
 2 small zucchini, sliced
 1 package (10 ounces) frozen whole-kernel corn,
    or 2 cups fresh corn
 2 large tomatoes, cut into chunks
 ¾ teaspoon cumin
 1 teaspoon salt
    Chopped parsley

Sauté the onion in butter in a large saucepan until the onion is soft but not browned. Stir in the raisins, zucchini, corn, tomatoes, cumin, and salt. (If the tomatoes are very firm or underripe, add 2 or 3 tablespoons water to the pan.) Slowly heat to a simmer. Stir gently, then simmer covered for 6 to 8 minutes, or until vegetables are tender. Stir gently and serve sprinkled with chopped parsley.

Asparagus Polonaise

Makes 4 to 6 servings
 1 hard-cooked egg, shelled
 ¼ cup parsley sprigs
 2 slices dry bread
 ¼ cup butter or margarine
 2 pounds asparagus or 2 packages (10 ounces
    each) frozen asparagus, cooked, drained, and
    kept hot

Start blender at medium speed. While blender is running, tip center cap and add egg, blending until chopped. Empty into small bowl. Start blender at medium speed. While blender is running, tip center cap and add parsley, blending until chopped. Stir into chopped egg. Break bread into blender container. Cover; blend at medium speed until crumbled. Heat butter in small skillet. Add bread crumbs; cook over medium heat, stirring occasionally, until golden brown. Combine with egg mixture; sprinkle over asparagus.
Note: Crumb topping may also be used with broccoli or cauliflower.

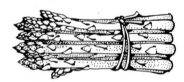

Baked Green Beans

Makes 4 servings
 1 pound green beans
 3 slices bacon, diced
 1 large onion, chopped
 1 cup sliced mushrooms
 1 can (10½ ounces) Campbell's Condensed
    Chicken Broth
 ¼ teaspoon pepper

Remove ends of green beans. Wash and drain beans; arrange in a shallow casserole. In skillet fry bacon until crisp. Add onions and mushrooms; sauté until wilted but not brown. Stir in remaining ingredients. Pour over green beans. Bake covered in a preheated 350°F. oven for 40 to 45 minutes or until beans are easily pierced. Remove from oven. If desired, liquid in casserole may be thickened with 2 teaspoons cornstarch mixed with 2 tablespoons water. Cook until broth is thickened.

Bean Sprouts with Mushrooms and Celery

Makes 8 servings
 ¼ cup peanut oil
 1 cup sliced celery
 2 small onions, sliced
 12 small mushrooms, sliced
 1 can (10½ ounces) Campbell's Condensed
    Chicken Broth
 2 tablespoons soy sauce
 2 cans (16 ounces each) bean sprouts, drained
 1 tablespoon cornstarch
 ¼ cup cold water

Heat peanut oil in a skillet and sauté celery, onions, and mushrooms until wilted. Add chicken broth and soy sauce. Add bean sprouts, bring to a boil and boil for 1 minute. Mix cornstarch and water. Stir mixture quickly into bean sprouts. Cook, stirring, until broth bubbles and thickens.

Crunchy Green Bean Bake

Makes about 4 servings
 1 can (16 ounces) green beans, drained
 1 jar (2½ ounces) sliced mushrooms, drained
 ⅓ cup Wish-Bone® Chunky Blue Cheese Dressing
    Canned French fried onions

Preheat oven to 350°F. In 1-quart casserole, combine all ingredients, except onions; bake covered 10 minutes. Top with onions; bake uncovered an additional 5 minutes, or until onions are heated.

Green Beans Imperial

Makes about 6 servings

> 2 packages (9 ounces each) frozen green beans
> 1 envelope Lipton® Onion-Mushroom Recipe
>   Soup Mix
> ¼ cup whipping or heavy cream
> ¼ teaspoon dill weed

Cook beans according to package directions; do not drain. Stir in remaining ingredients; heat through, but do not boil.

Variation

Substitute parsley for the dill weed.

Green Beans Français

Makes about 3 servings

> 1 package (10 ounces) frozen green beans
> ¼ cup Wish-Bone® Deluxe French Dressing
>   Buttered bread crumbs

Cook green beans according to package directions; drain. Toss with Wish-Bone Deluxe French Dressing and top with bread crumbs.

Variation

Try 1 package (10 ounces) frozen broccoli or asparagus spears.

Baked Beans

Makes 8 servings

> 1 pound navy pea beans
> 2 onions, chopped
> ½ cup firmly packed brown sugar
> ½ cup molasses
> 1½ teaspoons salt
> ¾ teaspoon dry mustard
> 6 slices bacon, diced

Rinse beans well. Pick over and rinse again. Place in 3- or 4-quart casserole. Add 4½ cups water. Cover and let stand at least several hours, or overnight. Do not drain. Cover casserole. Bake at 350°F. 1 hour. Stir in remaining ingredients, cover, and bake 1 hour and 30 minutes. Stir and bake uncovered 1 hour, or until beans are tender and glazed.

Bean Cooking Magic

There are almost as many "favorite" methods for preparing beans as there are cooks. To clear up the confusion, the California Bean Board and USDA scientists carried on ten years of research to develop a *best* way. For the best combination of flavor, digestibility, and nutrition, follow these steps:

Step 1: Buy good beans. Look for firm, clean, whole beans of uniform size and color. Stick with a brand you like for consistent quality.

Step 2: Wash and sort. Rinse dry beans in cold water; remove damaged beans and any foreign material.

Step 3: Soak. For each pound (2 cups) washed, sorted dry beans, add 6 to 8 cups hot water in a pot large enough to permit expansion. Boil 3 minutes; cover and soak 1 to 4 hours, adding water as needed to keep beans covered. Drain off soak water and rinse.

Step 4: Cook. Put soaked, drained, and rinsed beans (1 pound dry makes 4 to 6 cups cooked beans) into a 3- to 4-quart pot with 6 cups hot water, 2 tablespoons shortening, 2 teaspoons salt. Boil gently until desired tenderness is reached (depending on variety, usually 1 to 2 hours).

Preparation notes: In recipes calling for slow, all-day cooking, soaking is not essential, but soaking shortens cooking time. And, when you use the boil-soak method (step 3), the taste, texture, appearance, and digestibility of the beans are improved. For even better digestibility, also discard the cook water. Tests show no important amounts of essential nutrients are lost.

Cooking time: Cooking time depends on intended use, bean variety, storage conditions, altitude, water softness, and if they're cooked with acids. These tips will help you judge cooking time and desired tenderness:

- **Intended Use.** Beans are better firm for salads and when beans will be cooked further in casseroles, soups, or stews. To purée or mash, cook until soft.
- **Variety.** Colored and dappled beans generally take longer to cook than white. (Exceptions: small whites and garbanzos.) Black-eyes usually cook most quickly.
- **Storage.** Dry beans stored at high temperature and humidity for long periods are difficult to cook. Store in a cool, dry place.
- **Altitude.** At high altitudes water boils at lower temperatures so beans take longer to cook.
- **Water Softness.** Add ⅛ to ¼ teaspoon baking soda (no more) per pound of beans to shorten cooking time in hard water.
- **Cooked with Acids.** Acid foods slow down cooking. Add tomatoes, vinegar, etc., last.

Baked Beans (page 93). Caloric Corporation

Green Beans Vinaigrette

Makes 4 servings
- ¾ cup vegetable or olive oil
- ¼ cup lemon juice or red wine vinegar
- ½ teaspoon dry mustard
- ½ teaspoon salt
  Dash pepper
- 6 parsley sprigs
- 1 tablespoon cut-up fresh chervil leaves or 1 teaspoon dried chervil
- 1 tablespoon cut-up fresh chives
- ½ canned pimiento, cut up
- 1 pound fresh green beans or 2 packages (10 ounces each) frozen green beans, cooked and drained

Put all ingredients except green beans into blender container in order listed. Cover; blend at medium speed until herbs and pimiento are chopped. Pour into small saucepan; heat to lukewarm. Pour over green beans. Serve hot or let stand 1 hour, stirring once or twice, and serve.

Asparagus Vinaigrette

Substitute cooked asparagus for green beans. Proceed as for Green Beans Vinaigrette.

Clustered Bean and Corn Salad

Makes 8 servings
- 1 can (1 pound 4 ounces) red kidney beans, drained
- 1 can (1 pound) whole-kernel corn, drained
- 1 package (9 ounces) frozen cut green beans, cooked and drained
- ½ cup oil
- 2 tablespoons Lea & Perrins Worcestershire Sauce
- 2 tablespoons wine vinegar
- 1 teaspoon prepared brown mustard
- ¾ teaspoon salt
- ½ teaspoon sugar
- ½ teaspoon curry powder
  Lettuce (optional)

In a large serving bowl, arrange kidney beans, corn, and green beans in clusters; set aside. In a small container, combine remaining ingredients; mix well. Pour over vegetables. Cover and refrigerate for 2 hours or longer. Serve on lettuce-lined salad plates, if desired.

Asparagus Polonaise (page 92). Hamilton Beach Scovill Inc.

Baked Vegetable Macedoine (page 75). Lea & Perrins.

Green Beans Italian

Makes 5 servings

> 3 tablespoons Land O Lakes Sweet Cream Butter
> ½ medium-size onion, cut into ¼-inch rings (½ cup)
> 1 package (9 ounces) frozen cut green beans, thawed and drained
> 2 tablespoons ripe olives, sliced ⅛ inch thick
> 1 teaspoon basil leaves
> ½ teaspoon salt
> ⅛ teaspoon garlic powder
> ½ cup medium-size tomato, cut in ½ inch cubes (½ cup)

In 2-quart saucepan, melt butter. Stir in onion. Cook uncovered over medium heat, stirring occcasionally, until crisp-tender, 3 to 5 minutes. Stir in remaining ingredients *except* tomato. Cover; continue cooking, stirring occasionally, until vegetables are crisp-tender, 5 to 7 minutes. Stir in tomato. Cover; continue cooking 1 minute.

Broccoli Waldorf

Makes about 4 servings

> 1 package (10 ounces) frozen broccoli spears
> ⅓ cup coarsely chopped walnuts
> 1 apple, diced
> ¼ cup Wish-Bone® Sweet 'n Spicy French Dressing
> ¼ cup plain yogurt
> 1 tablespoon honey

Cook broccoli according to package directions; drain. Add remaining ingredients; heat through.

Elegant Puffed Broccoli

Makes 6 to 8 servings

> 2 bunches broccoli, cut into spears, or 2 packages (10 ounces each) frozen broccoli spears, cooked and drained
> 2 egg whites, at room temperature
> ¼ teaspoon salt
> ½ cup shredded Swiss cheese (2 ounces)
> ½ cup Hellmann's or Best Foods Real Mayonnaise

Arrange cooked broccoli in shallow 1½-quart pan or broiler-proof serving dish. In small bowl, with mixer at high speed, beat egg whites and salt until stiff peaks form. Fold in cheese and mayonnaise until well blended. Spoon evenly over broccoli. Broil 6 inches from source of heat 4 minutes, or until golden brown. Serve immediately.

Broccoli Basics

Wash under cold running water. Remove largest leaves, and any others that are blemished. With a sharp knife, cut a deep cross in the bottom of each stalk—heads cook faster than stalks; the cross allows the water to reach into the stalk, assuring that both heads and stalks will be done at the same time. Or, if you prefer, slice the entire stalk lengthwise, with one floweret and a thin piece of stalk in each cut. Cook in a large, flat pan—a skillet is ideal, provided it has a cover—in an inch of water until barely tender, 10 to 15 minutes. Cover, but remove cover briefly several times during the cooking period. This allows excess steam to escape, and helps keep the broccoli green. Drain well before serving.

An alternative method is to cut off the heads and cut the stalks into 1-inch slices. Cook the stalk slices 5 minutes; add the heads and continue cooking until done.

Broccoli may also be cooked by the stir-fry method. Cut in thin slices and sauté quickly in hot oil, again cooking the stalk sections a bit longer than the heads.

To serve simply, dress with butter, salt, and pepper. Or drizzle with melted butter, sprinkle with cheese, and broil briefly until the cheese melts. Or dress with lemon butter or with hollandaise sauce. Or sprinkle with crumbled crisp bacon. Cooked in advance and refrigerated, cold broccoli is delicious as an appetizer or salad, with vinaigrette or simply with lemon juice, or mayonnaise thinned with lemon juice and sharpened with Cayenne, or with sour cream. Use leftover broccoli to make a delicious cream soup. And, of course, broccoli is the base for chicken or turkey divan—broccoli topped with breast slices of poultry, napped with a sherry-flavored cream sauce, sprinkled with Parmesan, and baked until bubbling hot and lightly browned.

Broccoli with Mornay Sauce

Makes 3 cups sauce

> ¼ cup butter or margarine
> ¼ cup all-purpose flour
> 1½ cups whole-milk yogurt
> 2 teaspoons Steero Instant Chicken Bouillon or 2 Steero cubes dissolved in 1 cup water
> ½ cup grated Parmesan or romano cheese
> ½ cup shredded Swiss cheese
> 1 large bunch broccoli, cooked

Melt butter in a small saucepan and blend in the flour. Stir in yogurt and blend until thickened. Add 1 cup Steero bouillon and cheeses and stir over low heat until cheeses melt. Serve over hot, cooked broccoli.

Broccoli au Gratin

Makes 4 servings
- 1 slice dry bread, buttered
- ½ cup cubed Swiss cheese
- 1 cup Medium White Sauce (recipe follows)
- 1 bunch broccoli or 2 packages (10 ounces each) frozen broccoli, cooked and drained

Break bread into blender container. Cover; blend at medium speed until crumbled. Empty onto wax paper; set aside. Start blender at medium speed. While blender is running, tip center cap and gradually add cheese, blending until grated. Empty onto another sheet of wax papper; set aside. Prepare Medium White Sauce. Heat oven to 375°F. Put half the broccoli into buttered 1-quart baking dish. Add half the sauce; sprinkle with half the Swiss cheese. Repeat layers. Sprinkle top with bread crumbs. Bake 15 to 20 minutes or until bubbly and golden brown.

Variations

Asparagus or cauliflowerets may be used in place of broccoli. Cheddar cheese may be substituted for Swiss cheese. If desired, grated Parmesan cheese may be mixed with bread crumbs for topping.

Medium White Sauce

Makes 1 cup sauce
- 1 cup milk
- 2 tablespoons softened butter or margarine
- 2 tablespoons all-purpose flour
- ¼ teaspoon salt
- Dash pepper

Put all ingredients into blender container in order listed. Cover; blend at high speed until smooth. Pour into small saucepan. Cook over medium heat, stirring constantly, until mixture thickens and comes to a boil.

Thin White Sauce

Prepare Medium White Sauce using 1 tablespoon butter and 1 tablespoon flour.

Thick White Sauce

Prepare Medium White Sauce using 3 tablespoons butter and 3 tablespoons flour.

Brussels Sprouts with Chestnuts

Makes 8 servings
- 3 cups cooked brussels sprouts
- ¾ pound cooked chestnuts
- Salt and pepper to taste
- Butter
- Beef bouillon
- Fine dry bread crumbs
- Paprika

Oil a 2-quart casserole. Fill with alternate layers of sprouts and chestnuts, seasoning each layer lightly with salt and pepper and dotting each layer with butter. Moisten lightly with bouillon. Sprinkle heavily with bread crumbs. Dot with butter; sprinkle with paprika. Bake in a preheated 350°F. oven for 30 minutes.

Consider Brussels Sprouts Tonight

Low in sodium, brussels sprouts are a good vegetable to keep in mind if you're cooking for someone on a low-salt diet. They're low in calories, too, and high in vitamins A and C. A cup of brussels sprouts—7 or 8 individual heads—contains about 55 calories.

To cook, cut off stalk from each sprout, but not so close to the head that you loosen the leaves. Pull off any yellowed or blemished leaves. Wash in deep cold water. Cook covered in a small amount of water, 5 to 10 minutes, or until just tender. Overcooked, brussels sprouts lose vitamins and their flavor is intensified to the unpleasant point.

Dress cooked sprouts with butter, lemon-butter, browned butter, cheese sauce, hollandaise, or sour cream. Combine with mushrooms, chestnuts (a traditional holiday vegetable), water chestnuts, almonds, or crisp croutons for texture contrast. Season with black or white pepper, lemon-parsley salt, nutmeg, dill. Serve whole sprouts, cooked tender-crisp and chilled, with a mustard dip or vinaigrette sauce as an appetizer. Bake with potatoes in cheese sauce. Skewer with lamb chunks and tomato wedges for kebabs. Serve on toast, topped with creamed eggs.

Brussels Sprouts Cheddar

Makes 6 to 8 servings
- 2 pounds brussels sprouts
- 1 can (10¾ ounces) Campbell's Condensed Cheddar Cheese Soup
- Dash Worcestershire sauce
- 2 drops Tabasco pepper sauce
- Dash Cayenne pepper
- Paprika

Wash and trim brussels sprouts. Cut sprouts into halves and cook in boiling salted water to cover until sprouts are tender, but still firm and slightly crisp. Combine soup, Worcestershire sauce, Tabasco sauce, and Cayenne. Place well-drained sprouts in a shallow baking dish. Spoon soup mixture over sprouts. Sprinkle with paprika. Place under broiler until lightly browned.

Baked Sweet 'n' Sour Brussels Sprouts

Makes 4 servings★

    1 package (10 ounces) frozen brussels sprouts
    ⅓ cup liquid Butter Buds, divided
    2 tablespoons cider vinegar
    1½ teaspoons sugar
    ¼ teaspoon tarragon
    ⅛ teaspoon marjoram
    ⅛ teaspoon freshly ground pepper
    ⅓ cup sliced fresh mushrooms
    1 tablespoon chopped pimiento

Preheat oven to 350°F. Cook brussels sprouts in small amount of unsalted water just until thawed. Drain. Arrange sprouts in shallow baking dish. Combine 4 tablespoons Butter Buds, vinegar, sugar, tarragon, marjoram, and pepper in blender container. Cover and process on medium speed a few seconds. Pour over sprouts. Combine remaining Butter Buds, mushrooms, and pimiento. Sprinkle over sprouts. Bake covered about 15 minutes, or until sprouts are tender.
★Each serving contains 45 calories and 8 gm carbohydrate. By using Butter Buds instead of butter in this recipe, you will save 125 calories and 70 mg cholesterol per serving. You can also substitute ½ packet Sweet 'N Low for the sugar in this recipe. You'll save 5 calories and 1 gm carbohydrate per serving.

Baked Sweet 'n' Sour Brussels Sprouts. Courtesy of Butter Buds

Cranberry Acorn Squash (page 116). The Reynolds Wrap Kitchen

Green Beans Italian (page 96). Land O' Lakes, Inc.

Creamed Cabbage

Makes 6 servings
   1 medium head green cabbage, coarsely cut up
   1 thin slice onion
   ¼ cup milk
   2 tablespoons softened butter or margarine
   2 tablespoons all-purpose flour
   1 teaspoon salt
   ⅛ teaspoon pepper
   ¼ teaspoon caraway seed (optional)

Fill blender container to the 5-cup mark with cabbage. Add water just to cover cabbage. Cover; blend at medium speed until coarsely chopped. Drain thoroughly in colander; empty into saucepan. Repeat process with remaining cabbage. Put remaining ingredients except caraway seed into blender container in order listed. Cover; blend at high speed until smooth. Add to cabbage; mix thoroughly. Cook over low heat, stirring frequently, 10 to 12 minutes, or until cabbage is just tender. Sprinkle with caraway seed, if desired.

Pennsylvania Red Cabbage

Makes 6 servings
   1 medium head red cabbage
   ½ teaspoon caraway seed
   ½ cup vinegar
   ½ cup brown sugar
   1½ teaspoons salt
      Dash pepper
   2 medium apples, cored and cut in quarters
   2 tablespoons salad oil or bacon drippings

Blender-chop cabbage. Empty into a saucepan and add caraway seed. Put ½ cup water and the remaining ingredients into blender. Cover and process at Chop until apples are coarsely chopped. Pour over cabbage. Simmer covered 1 hour.

Hot Cabbage Slaw

Makes 6 servings
   ⅓ cup water
   2 beef bouillon cubes
   1 medium-size (about 1½ pounds) green
      cabbage, coarsely shredded
   ½ cup chopped onion
   ½ cup grated carrot
   2 tablespoons wine vinegar
   2 teaspoons Lea & Perrins Worcestershire Sauce
   ½ teaspoon caraway seed

In a large saucepan, combine water and bouillon cubes. Bring to boiling point, stirring to dissolve bouillon cubes. Add cabbage. Reduce heat and simmer covered for 10 minutes. Add remaining ingredients; simmer covered until cabbage is tender, about 10 minutes longer.

Baked Carrot Puffs

Makes 6 to 8 servings
   2 pounds carrots, pared and sliced
   1 teaspoon salt
      Graham crackers
   6 tablespoons butter or margarine, divided
      Dash ground ginger
   2 eggs, separated
   ¼ cup light brown sugar
   ¼ cup fine dry bread crumbs

Preheat oven to 375°F. Cook carrots with ½ cup water and salt for about 15 minutes, or until tender. Break a few graham crackers into blender. Cover and process at Crumb. Empty crumbs into a measuring cup. Continue until there is ¾ cup graham cracker crumbs. Empty into large bowl of Sunbeam Mixmaster Mixer. Drain liquid from cooked carrots. Place carrots in blender. Cover and process at Purée until smooth. Turn into large bowl of Mixer. Add 4 tablespoons of the butter, ginger and egg yolks. Beat at low speed until smooth. Cool. Beat egg whites in small bowl of Mixmaster Mixer at highest speed until they form peaks. Fold into carrot mixture. Turn mixture into a 3-quart casserole. Combine remaining 2 tablespoons butter with brown sugar and bread crumbs. Sprinkle over top. Bake 40 minutes.

English-Style Self-Sauce Vegetables

Cook four servings of the vegetable of your choice, cut into bite-size pieces, in 1 cup boiling water. Drain, reserving the cooking liquid. Place vegetables in a serving dish and keep warm; return liquid to cooking pan. Cream together 2 tablespoons softened butter or margarine and 2 tablespoons all-purpose flour until well combined. With the cooking liquid at a slow boil, stir in butter mixture a small piece at a time; cook 1 minute after mixture is all used. Season to taste with salt, pepper, and an herb or spice of your choice. Pour over vegetables and serve at once.

Carrots in Cream and Dill

Makes 6 servings

- 1 **bunch carrots**
- 1 **cup sliced onions**
- 1 **clove garlic, minced**
- ¼ **cup olive oil**
- 1 **tablespoon all-purpose flour**
- 1 **can (10½ ounces) Campbell's Condensed**
  Cream of Celery Soup
- 1 **cup milk**
- ½ **teaspoon dill seed or 1 tablespoon chopped dill**
- 1 **teaspoon sugar**
  Salt, pepper, and allspice

Scrape carrots and cut into julienne strips. Sauté carrots, onions, and garlic in oil for 5 minutes. Sprinkle with flour. Stir in soup and milk. Add dill and sugar. Simmer until carrots are tender, about 25 minutes, stirring occasionally. Season to taste with salt, pepper, and allspice.

Sweet 'n' Spicy Glazed Carrots

Makes about 4 servings

- 2 **tablespoons Wish-Bone® Sweet 'n Spicy French**
  Dressing
- 2 **tablespoons brown sugar**
- 1 **can (15 ounces) whole carrots, drained**

In small skillet, blend Wish-Bone Sweet 'n Spicy French Dressing with brown sugar; heat until bubbling. Add carrots and cook, stirring constantly, until glazed, about 5 minutes.

Sautéed Carrots

Makes 4 servings

- 8 **carrots**
- ¼ **teaspoon salt**
  Sugar
- ¼ **cup butter or margarine**

Scrape carrots and cut in half lengthwise. Cook until almost tender in small amount of boiling salted water. Drain on rack. Dip in sugar. Preheat Sunbeam Multi-Cooker Frypan to 300°F. Add butter and melt. Add carrots; sautée to golden color, turning frequently.

Secrets to Vegetable Cookery

Prepare vegetables immediately before cooking; cook them quickly and serve them promptly to retain maximum flavor and nutritive value.

Discover the variety of ways vegetables can be cooked:

Boil them in ½ to 1 inch of boiling, salted water until tender-crisp.

Steam them in a steamer basket set over rapidly boiling water just until tender-crisp. (They may also be steamed in a small amount of water in a covered casserole set in a 350°F. oven. Cooked in this way, vegetables take about 2 to 3 times longer than boiling.)

Bake them on the oven rack on a baking sheet or in a shallow casserole.

Braise them in a covered skillet or saucepan with about 2 tablespoons butter, margarine, or drippings, and 1 or 2 tablespoons water. Cooked in this way, vegetables are also known as "panned."

Broil tender, raw vegetables, such as tomatoes and mushrooms, brushed with butter or margarine.

Fry or stir-fry them in a small amount of fat over medium heat or **French-fry** them in hot, deep fat.

Pressure cook or steam them under pressure, following manufacturer's directions.

Orange Carrots

Makes 6 servings

- 1 **tablespoon unsalted margarine**
- 3 **cups diagonally thinly sliced carrots**
- 3 **scallions, cut into ½-inch pieces**
- ¼ **teaspoon Nu-Salt**
- ⅛ **teaspoon ground ginger**
- ⅛ **teaspoon ground cinnamon**
  Dash ground red pepper
- 3 **tablespoons water**
- 1 **can (11 ounces) mandarin oranges, drained,**
  reserving ¼ cup juice
- 1½ **teaspoons cornstarch**

In large nonstick skillet, melt margarine. Add carrots, scallions, Nu-Salt, ginger, cinnamon, and red pepper; cook and stir about 5 minutes. Add water, simmer 3 to 5 minutes. In bowl, mix reserved juice and cornstarch. Add cornstarch mixture and oranges to skillet; cook about 1 minute.

Celery and Almonds

Makes 6 servings
- 2 **tablespoons almonds**
- 4 **tablespoons olive oil**
- 1½ **cups water**
- **Salt to taste**
- 3 **cups celery (1 bunch, washed and cut into 1½-inch lengths)**
- 1 **tablespoon lemon juice**
- 1 **large potato, quartered and parboiled**

Blanch and drain almonds. When dry, brown in 2 tablespoons hot olive oil in small skillet. Bring 1½ cups water and remaining olive oil to a boil. Add salt, celery, and lemon juice, and simmer for 15 minutes. Then add the potato and almonds and cook 15 to 20 minutes longer. Serve hot.

Celery and Chestnuts

Makes 8 servings
- ½ **pound Italian chestnuts**
- 4 **tablespoons olive oil**
- **Salt to taste**
- 3 **cups celery (1 bunch, washed and cut into 1½-inch lengths)**
- 1 **tablespoon lemon juice**
- 1 **large potato, quartered and parboiled**

Cut a cross into flat side of chestnuts; sprinkle with water. Spread in flat pan and roast in hot oven for 20 minutes. While they are roasting, prepare liquid. To 1½ cups water and olive oil, which have been brought to a boil, add salt, celery, and lemon juice. Then remove shells from chestnuts, cut in half, and add, together with potato, to above mixture. Simmer for about 20 minutes longer. When celery is done, remove. Reduce liquid to a light gravy texture. Serve hot.

Basic Herbed Lemon Butter

Makes ¼ cup butter
- ¼ **cup butter**
- 1 **teaspoon freshly grated lemon peel**
- 1 **tablespoon freshly squeezed lemon juice**
- ½ **teaspoon of 1 or more of the following: parsley, marjoram, oregano, minced onion, tarragon, paprika, or 1 teaspoon dill weed or basil**

Melt butter; add lemon peel and juice, blending well. Add any 1 of the seasonings or a combination, if desired. Keep warm while preparing vegetables.

Basic Herbed Lemon Butter on vegetables. Courtesy of Sunkist Growers, Inc.

Lemon Butter Patties

Use Basic Herbed Lemon Butter ingredients, creaming butter, then adding lemon peel and juice. Stir in parsley and add any other desired seasoning. Shape into 1x5-inch roll. Place in refrigerator to harden. Slice roll into 8 butter pats and serve on vegetables.

Lemon-Broiled Tomatoes

- **Basic Herbed Lemon Butter**
- ¼ **cup soft bread crumbs**
- 3 **large tomatoes, cut in half**

Use Basic Herbed Lemon Butter ingredients, creaming butter, then adding lemon peel and juice. Stir in desired seasoning and bread crumbs. Spread mixture on tomato halves and broil until lightly browned.

Lemon Stuffed Mushrooms

- **Basic Herbed Lemon Butter**
- ½ **cup soft bread crumbs**
- 20 **large mushroom caps, rinsed, drained**
- ¼ **cup hot water**

Use Basic Herbed Lemon Butter ingredients, creaming butter, then adding lemon peel and juice. Stir in desired seasoning and bread crumbs. Spoon mixture into mushroom caps. Place in shallow baking pan, filling side up. Pour in water and bake for 15 minutes at 375°F.

Herbed Orange Butter

Substitute same amonts orange peel and juice for lemon peel and juice. Add desired seasoning. Excellent on carrots.

Sweet 'n' Spicy Glazed Carrots (page 101); Sautéed Carrots (page 101)

Fruited Celery

Makes 6 servings

- 1 **stalk celery**
- 3 **tablespoons butter or margarine**
- ⅓ **cup chopped onion**
- 1 **apple, diced**
- ½ **cup golden raisins**
- 1 **tablespoon Lea & Perrins Worcestershire Sauce**
- 1¼ **teaspoons salt**

Separate celery into ribs; cut off leaves (save for soups and stews). Slice ribs diagonally into 1-inch pieces (makes about 6 cups). In a large skillet, melt butter. Add onion and celery; sauté until tender, about 5 minutes. Mix in apple, raisins, Lea & Perrins, and salt; stir-fry until celery is crisp-tender, about 5 minutes.

Sweet-Corn Custard

Makes 8 servings

- 3 **cups (about 8 ears) fresh corn, scraped from the cob**
- 2 **tablespoons all-purpose flour**
- 1½ **teaspoons sugar**
- 1 **cup light cream**
- **Salt and white pepper to taste**
- **Butter**

Score the ears of corn by running a knife lengthwise through the rows of kernels. With the dull edge of the knife, scrape corn from the cobs, removing all milky pulp. Mix flour and sugar with corn. Stir in cream gradually. Season lightly with salt and pepper. Generously oil a 9-inch square baking dish. Pour in corn mixture. Dot the top with butter. Bake in a preheated 325°F. oven for 1 hour, or until lightly browned and set.

Broiled Eggplant Japanese Style

Makes 4 servings

- 1 **eggplant (about 1 pound)**
- ¼ **cup vegetable oil**
- 2 **tablespoons Kikkoman Soy Sauce**
- 2 **tablespoons ginger juice★**

Cut eggplant crosswise into ½-inch-thick slices. Combine remaining ingredients in large shallow baking pan. Add eggplant; turn pieces over to coat both sides. Marinate in single layer 15 minutes; turn over occasionally. Remove slices; arrange in single layer on large baking sheet. Broil 4 minutes; turn slices and broil 4 minutes longer, or until tender. Serve immediately.

★Press enough fresh ginger root pieces through garlic press to measure 2 tablespoons.

Fennel Braisé

Makes 4 servings

> 1 strip bacon, chopped
> ¼ cup marrow (4 pieces marrow bone, about 2 inches long)
> 1 can (10½ ounces) Campbell's Condensed French Onion Soup
> 1 carrot, chopped
> 1 tablespoon chopped parsley
> 2 bunches fennel, trimmed and cut into 4-inch strips
> Salt and pepper

Combine bacon, marrow, onion soup, carrot, and parsley in a large saucepan. Bring to a boil, lower heat, and simmer. Trim fennel until only green stalks and white stalks remain. Add fennel to simmering broth. Toss to coat, cover tightly, and simmer for 15 minutes, or until fennel is crisp-tender. Season to taste.

Deviled Leeks

Makes 4 to 6 servings

> 6 large leeks
> ¼ cup butter or margarine, melted, divided
> ⅓ cup chicken broth or water
> ¼ cup dry white wine
> 1 teaspoon salt
> ⅛ teaspoon freshly ground pepper
> 2 teaspoons Dijon mustard
> ½ teaspoon thyme
> 1 cup fresh bread crumbs

Clean leeks; cut lengthwise into 4 pieces, then crosswise into 1-inch strips. Place in 1½-quart casserole. Combine 2 tablespoons butter, chicken broth, wine, salt, and pepper. Pour over leeks; set aside. Combine remaining butter, mustard, and thyme. Add bread crumbs to butter mixture and toss lightly to mix. Sprinkle crumb mixture over leeks. Preheat oven to 350°F. Cover casserole and bake 20 minutes. Remove cover and bake 5 to 6 minutes until topping is lightly browned and leeks are tender.

Mushrooms à la Russe

Makes 6 servings

> 2 pounds mushrooms
> Juice of ½ lemon
> 2 cans (10½ ounces each) Campbell's Condensed Cream of Mushroom Soup
> 1 tablespoon butter
> ⅓ cup heavy cream
> ⅓ cup sour cream
> Salt and pepper
> Toast or biscuits

Wash mushrooms, drain, and slice. Cover with water, add lemon juice, and simmer until mushrooms are tender, about 10 minutes. Drain. Combine soup, butter, heavy cream, and sour cream. Heat until bubbly. Fold in sliced mushrooms. Reheat and season to taste with salt and pepper. Serve spooned over toast or split hot biscuits.

Mushroom Magic

There are thousands of ways to enjoy mushrooms. To prepare them, first wipe with a damp paper towel—never wash in a large amount of water, and never soak them in water. To remove stems, twist gently; if you leave stems in place, cut off and discard a thin slice from the bottoms. Cut stems off even with caps if the mushrooms are to be stuffed—that remaining stub of stem helps the mushroom hold its shape nicely during cooking. And never peel mushrooms; the thin skins hold a part of the flavor—and the nutrients—and help the mushrooms keep their shape in cooking. If you need further convincing, peeled mushrooms darken more easily than unpeeled ones.

In whatever way you cook mushrooms, make the cooking time brief. If you sauté them, sliced, 3 to 4 minutes is ample. To cook them to add to such dishes as casseroles, place in a pan with ¼ inch water. Cover pan and cook over medium-high heat 2 to 3 minutes, until the mushrooms have expressed their liquid; uncover and continue to cook until the liquid is somewaht evaporated, another 2 minutes or so. Use the liquid, full of good mushroom flavor, in making sauce. A little lemon juice added during cooking will keep the mushrooms from turning dark.

Freezing mushrooms: Although mushrooms are available all year around, they are less plentiful—and so, more expensive—in the summer, making winter mushrooms a practical freezer item. Freeze small mushrooms whole, quarter larger ones. Steam-blanch 3 to 5 minutes, depending on size; chill, drain, pack, and freeze. Or sauté in butter 2 minutes; pack, pouring butter from the skillet over the mushrooms; freeze. Add lemon juice to the sautéed mushrooms, citric or ascorbic acid to the blanched ones, to prevent darkening.

Other ways, other forms: Although fresh mushrooms are virtually always to be had, other forms are available. Dried mushrooms are black and rather off-putting to look at until you know their secret—superb flavor; rehydrate in warm water before using.

Freeze-dried diced mushrooms are in jars, but not widely distributed; cooking rehydrates them without previous soaking—good flavor for cooked dishes and sauces. Mushrooms are also available in cans or jars or in the frozen-food section of your supermarket.

Deviled Leeks (page 105). Caloric Corporation

Apple-Onion Bake (page 107). Caloric Corporation

Creamed Cabbage (page 100)

Baked Mushroom Crisp

Makes 4 to 6 servings

    ¼ cup butter or margarine
    2½ cups (½ pound) sliced mushrooms
    2 cups croutons
    1 cup light cream
    1½ tablespoons Lea & Perrins Worcestershire Sauce
    ¼ teaspoon salt

In a medium skillet, melt butter. Add mushrooms and sauté until golden, about 5 minutes. In a buttered 8-inch square baking pan, arrange alternate layers of mushrooms and croutons, ending with croutons. Combine cream, Lea & Perrins, and salt; pour over mushrooms and croutons. Bake in a preheated hot oven (425°F.) until top is golden brown, about 20 minutes.

Sautéed Mushrooms

Makes 4 servings

    ¼ cup butter or margarine
    1 tablespoon grated onion (optional)
    1 pound fresh mushrooms, sliced
      Salt and pepper
      Lemon juice

Preheat Sunbeam Multi-Cooker Frypan to 340°F. Add butter and melt. Add the onion and sauté a few minutes; then add mushrooms. Sauté, stirring frequently, about 5 to 8 minutes. Sprinkle with salt, pepper and lemon juice.

Almond Mushrooms

Makes 1½ dozen

    1 pound (about 1½ dozen) large mushrooms
    ½ cup fine dry bread crumbs
    2 teaspoons lemon juice
    ⅛ teaspoon rosemary
    ⅛ teaspoon marjoram
    ¼ teaspoon salt
    ¼ cup finely chopped blanched almonds
    1 tablespoon capers, drained (optional)
    3 tablespoons butter
    3 tablespoons finely snipped parsley

Wash mushrooms. Remove stems and reserve. Pat mushroom caps dry with paper towels. Chop mushroom stems very finely. Combine with bread crumbs, lemon juice, rosemary, marjoram, salt, almonds, and capers. Spoon mixture into mushroom caps. Place in an oiled shallow baking pan. Dot each mushroom with butter. Bake in a preheated 350°F. oven for 20 to 25 minutes. Sprinkle with parsley and serve immediately.

Apple-Onion Bake

Makes 4 to 6 servings

    2 apples, peeled and sliced
    2 onions, sliced
    ¼ cup firmly packed brown sugar
    ¼ cup raisins
    ½ teaspoon ground nutmeg
    ½ teaspoon salt
    ¼ cup apple juice
    1 tablespoon butter or margarine

Layer half of the apples in 1-quart casserole. Top with half of the onions. Combine brown sugar, raisins, nutmeg, and salt. Sprinkle half of the brown sugar mixture over onions. Repeat layers. Pour apple juice over ingredients in casserole and dot with butter. Cover casserole and bake at 350°F. 40 to 45 minutes, or until apples and onions are tender.

Golden Onions

Makes 4 to 6 servings

    3 tablespoons butter or margarine
    3 Spanish onions, sliced
    1 tablespoon curry powder (or to taste)

Heat Sunbeam Multi-Cooker Frypan to 320°F. Melt butter and add onions. Cook, turning often and breaking into rings, until tender and pale golden. Sprinkle with curry powder to taste before serving.

Cheese-Baked Onions

Makes 4 to 6 servings

    4 slices dry bread, buttered
    ½ cup cubed Swiss cheese
    2 cups Thin White Sauce (see index)
    2 pounds small white onions, peeled, cooked, and
        drained

Heat oven to 400°F. Break two slices bread into blender container. Cover; blend at medium speed until crumbed. Empty into bowl. Repeat process with remaining bread. Start blender at medium speed. While blender is running, tip center cap and gradually add cheese, blending until grated. Stir into bread crumbs. Prepare Thin White Sauce. Put onions into greased 1½-quart baking dish. Pour sauce over onions. Sprinkle with crumb mixture. Bake 15 minutes or until bubbly and golden brown.

Fabulous Onion Fries

Makes 4 to 6 servings

    1 envelope Lipton® Onion or Onion-Mushroom
        Recipe Soup Mix
    1 package (16 or 20 ounces) frozen French fried
        potatoes or potato rounds
    1 to 2 tablespoons oil

In large plastic bag, place Lipton Onion Recipe Soup Mix and potatoes; drizzle with oil. Shake vigorously until potatoes are well coated. Bake according to potato package directions.

French Fried Onion

    Large onions, sliced crosswise, ¼ inch thick
    All-purpose seasoned flour
    1 egg
    ¼ cup milk
    Fine dry bread crumbs
    Fat for deep frying
    Salt

Separate onion slices into rings and dip into seasoned flour, then into the egg beaten with the milk. Dip into crumbs and shake to remove excess. Fry in preheated shortening at 375°F. in Sunbeam Multi-Cooker Frypan until browned, about 3 minutes. Drain and place on paper towels. Sprinkle with salt; serve hot.

Onion Pilaf

Makes about 6 servings

  2 tablespoons butter or margarine
  ¾ cup chopped celery
1½ cups instant rice
1½ cups hot water
  1 envelope Lipton® Onion Recipe Soup Mix
  1 can (4 ounces) sliced mushrooms

In medium saucepan, melt butter and cook celery until tender. Stir in rice, water, Lipton Onion Recipe Soup Mix, and mushrooms. Bring to a boil, then simmer uncovered about 5 minutes.

Onions Without Tears

How to peel raw onions without weeping has been the subject of many a spirited discussion as well as assorted solemn magazine and cookbook articles, and there are almost as many old wives' tales on the subject as there are old wives. The consensus seems to be that what works for one will not necessarily work for everyone—or even anyone—else. Some people seem not to be much affected by the fumes. Others, courageous or masochistic as the case may be, simply go to it, grimly peeling and bitterly weeping until the job is done. Some mendaciously allow the youngsters to help Mommy by peeling the onions for her. Some, tossing liberation to the winds, cajole their spouses into doing the dirty work.

For what they are worth, here are some of the assorted onion-peeling helps that cooks have worked out; one or another of them may be just what you need:

> chew gum vigorously
> smoke a strong cigar (a somewhat damned-if-you-do/damned-if-you-don't solution)
> peel under running water (works for many)
> peel under standing water (same difference)
> hold a large crust of bread in your mouth as you peel
> start at the root end
> start at the stem end
> start in the middle and work both ways
> constantly dip your knife into water with lemon juice or vinegar added to it
> peel by an open window, with a fan behind you
> peel directly beneath the kitchen exhaust fan (requires a ladder for short women with high-placed fans)
> peel close to a solid room deodorizer
> light a candle (romatic but iffy)

Whatever turns off your tears.

Italian Sausage and Peppers

Makes 3 to 4 servings

1 pound Italian sausage (about 6 links)
1 large onion, sliced
¼ cup parsley, minced
1 can (16 ounces) tomatoes, puréed in blender
3 teaspoons Steero Instant Beef Bouillon or 3 Steero cubes dissolved in ½ cup of boiling water
⅛ teaspoon pepper
3 medium-size green peppers, seeded and sliced thin

Brown sausage links in skillet. Remove and set aside. Add onion to drippings and cook until tender. Cut sausage into 1-inch slices. Add to onion, stir in parsley, tomatoes, ½ cup Steero bouillon, and pepper. Simmer uncovered 30 minutes. Add green peppers. Cover and cook 15 minutes longer, or until peppers are tender.

Oriental-Style Self-Sauce Vegetables

Cook four servings of the vegetable of your choice, cut into bite-size pieces, in ¾ cup boiling water. Drain, reserving cooking liquid. Place vegetables in serving dish and keep warm; return liquid to cooking pan. Add ¼ teaspoon sugar, 2 tablespoons oil, 1 tablespoon rice vinegar, 1 teaspoon light soy sauce, and ½ teaspoon onion powder; bring to a boil. Dissolve 1 tablespoon cornstarch in 1 tablespoon cold water; add to liquid and cook 1 minute, stirring constantly. Pour over vegetables, toss lightly and serve at once.

Quick Pea Medley

Makes 4 servings

  2 tablespoons butter or margarine
  ¼ cup chopped onion
  ¼ cup chopped green pepper
  1 package (10 ounces) frozen peas
  1 can (8¼ ounces) tomatoes, broken up
1½ teaspoons Lea & Perrins Worcestershire Sauce
  ½ teaspoon salt

In a medium saucepan, melt butter. Add onion and green peppers; sauté for 3 minutes. Add peas, tomatoes, Lea & Perrins, and salt; mix gently. Bring to boiling point. Reduce heat and simmer uncovered for 5 minutes.

Mashed Potatoes

Makes 4 to 6 servings

    6 medium potatoes
    ⅓ to ⅔ cup hot milk or part cream
    2 to 3 tablespoons butter or margarine
    1 teaspoon salt
      Dash pepper, if desired

Pare potatoes and cook in boiling salted water until tender. Drain. Place over low heat for a few minutes to dry out, shaking frequently. When mealy, turn into large Sunbeam Mixmaster Mixer bowl. Beat at lowest speed, lifting beaters slightly, to chop potatoes, about 1 minute. Combine hot milk, butter, salt, and pepper. Pour over potatoes and whip at medium speed about 2 minutes, adding enough milk to make fluffy. Serve at once.

Potatoes au Gratin

Makes 6 servings

    4 cups thinly sliced peeled potatoes
    ¾ cup minced onions
    ¾ teaspoon salt
    1 can (11 ounces) condensed cheddar cheese soup
    ½ cup milk
    1 tablespoon Lea & Perrins Worcestershire Sauce

In a well-buttered 2-quart casserole, arrange potatoes, onions, and salt in alternate layers. Repeat three times. In a small saucepan, heat soup along with milk and Lea & Perrins. Pour over potato mixture. Cover. Bake in a preheated moderate oven (375 °F.) for 45 minutes. Remove cover and bake 15 minutes longer.

Scalloped Potatoes

Makes 6 servings

    3 slices bread, buttered
    1 small onion, cut up
    6 medium potatoes, pared and thinly sliced
    1 teaspoon salt
    ¼ teaspoon pepper
    1¾ cups milk

Heat oven to 350°F. Tear half the bread slices into blender container. Cover; blend at medium speed until crumbed. Empty onto wax paper; set aside. Repeat process with remaining bread. Put onion into blender container. Cover; blend at medium speed until chopped. Put one-third of potatoes in greased 1½-quart casserole; sprinkle with salt, pepper, one-third of onion, and one-third of crumbs. Repeat layers twice, ending with crumbs. Pour milk carefully down side of casserole so that top crumb layer is not disturbed. Bake covered 30 minutes. Uncover; bake 30 minutes longer.

Versatile Potato Cookery

Whenever you can, serve potatoes with their jackets still in place, and encourage your family to eat the skins—nutrients lurk there, and the skins provide diet-necessary fiber.

How to prepare. Scrub the vegetable gently under running water with a vegetable brush or kitchen sponge. Leave the skins on if you can; if you peel, use a swivel-blade vegetable parer to remove the thinnest possible amount of the skin. Peeled potatoes turn dark if not cooked immediately; put the pieces, as you peel them, into the water you will use for cooking. Cooked whole, potatoes retain maximum nutrients; however, if a shorter cooking time is wanted or if the recipe you are using requires it, slice, dice, or cube the potatoes.

To boil, use a heavy saucepan with a tight-fitting lid; cook in about 1 inch of (salted) water until tender, which should be 35 to 40 minutes for whole potatoes, 20 to 25 minutes for cut-up ones.

To steam (an excellent method of cooking potatoes), place a wire rack in the bottom of a kettle or large saucepan, add water to just below the level of the rack; bring to a boil, add potatoes, cook tightly covered until tender, which should take 30 to 45 minutes for whole potatoes, 20 to 30 for cut-up ones; if a rack is not available, improvise with crumpled foil in the bottom of the pan.

To rice, prepare boiled or steamed potatoes, drain and peel; force through a vegetable ricer or food mill; toss with melted butter before or after ricing, and season to taste.

To mash, prepare boiled or steamed potatoes, drain and peel; using a potato masher, electric mixer, or ricer, mash potatoes; gradually add heated milk, salt and white pepper to taste, and butter if you wish; beat until potatoes are smooth and fluffy.

To pan roast, prepare boiled or steamed potatoes, but cook only 10 minutes, drain and peel; arrange in a shallow baking pan, brush with melted butter or salad oil; bake uncovered at 400°F., about 45 minutes, or until fork-tender, turning occasionally; or arrange around meat in roasting pan, turn and baste with meat drippings frequently.

To bake, use an oven temperature of 400°F. if you are not baking anything else, but if you have another dish to bake, potatoes will tolerate any temperature from 325° to 450°—simply adjust the time to suit (at 400° the time should be about 45 minutes); pierce each potato several times with the tines of a fork before baking, to allow steam to escape and ensure that the potatoes won't burst; do not wrap in foil—that steams them, instead of baking.

Basic Baked Potatoes (page 111)

Duchess Potatoes

Makes 6 servings

> Packaged instant mashed potatoes for 6
>   servings
> Boiling water
> Milk
> 2 tablespoons butter or margarine
> ½ teaspoon salt
> ⅛ teaspoon ground nutmeg
> Dash Cayenne pepper
> 1 egg
> 2 egg yolks
> Melted butter or margarine

Heat oven to 450°F. or heat broiler. Following package directions for instant mashed potatoes, put half the amount of water and entire amount of milk specified on package into blender container. Add butter, salt, nutmeg, and Cayenne. Cover; blend at medium speed until mixed. While blender is running, tip center cap and add egg and egg yolks; add potatoes slowly; blend until smooth. Spoon in mounds or put through pastry tube onto greased cookie sheet. Brush with melted butter. Brown in oven or under broiler.

Q. *Why do potatoes turn green?*
A. They won't, if you store them in a dark place and use them within a week or so. This green tinge, which potatoes stored in the open or in see-through plastic bags will develop in 3 or 4 days, will spread with each passing day. The green color—indicating the presence of chlorophyll—is harmless in itself, but it is a signal that something harmful is taking place in the potato: the development of toxic substances, called glycoalkaloids, in the vegetable. These substances are always present in small amounts, but when potatoes turn green or sprout it is a sign that the levels of toxicity have doubled or tripled. Is the condition harmful? It can be. It can make most people ill; it even can be fatal to the few who are particularly sensitive to the glycoalkaloids. What to do? If the potatoes are deeply green or are beginning to shrivel, discard them. Otherwise, core out, with the point of a knife, the potato "eyes"; if there are any sprouts, treat them the same way. Then peel the potato deeply before cooking.

French Fries

Makes 6 servings

> 6 large potatoes, washed and peeled
> Ice water
> Peanut or corn oil for deep-fat frying
> Salt (optional)

Trim sides and ends of potatoes to form blocks. Cut lengthwise into ½-inch slices; stack slices evenly. Turn on side; slice again ½ inch wide. Soak in ice water for 20 minutes. Heat oil in deep-fat fryer (or 4 inches oil in large deep sauccpan) to 300°F. Drain potatoes; pat dry with paper towels. Place about 1 cup potatoes in fry basket or saucepan. Lower into oil. Deep-fat fry until potatoes are transparent but not browned. Remove basket from oil or use slotted spoon. Drain on paper towels. Just before serving, heat oil to 360°F. Deep fry, 1 cup potatoes at a time, until crisp and golden brown. Drain on paper towels. Sprinkle with salt, if desired. Serve immediately, or can be kept warm on oven.

Low-Calorie French Fries

Soak potatoes in ice water; drain; dry thoroughly on paper towels. Preheat oven to 450°F. Spread in single layer on jelly roll pan. Brush with 2 tablespoons vegetable oil. Shake pan to coat potatoes with oil. Bake until tender and golden brown, about 35 minutes. Sprinkle with salt, paprika, and pepper, if desired.
Makes 8 servings, about 100 calories per serving.

Basic Baked Potatoes

Makes 1 serving
> 1 or more large potatoes (6 to 8 ounces)

Preheat oven to 400°F. Scrub potatoes with brush in cold water; rinse well; dry with paper towels. For soft skins, rub with shortening or wrap in aluminum foil. For crisp skins, dry thoroughly. Pierce potatoes with fork. Place potatoes on oven rack or baking sheet. Bake 45 to 60 minutes, or until potatoes are easily pierced with fork. For perfect baked potatoes, gently roll back and forth on flat surface before serving. To serve, cut a cross in top of each potato; pinch to open. Top with any of the following: 1 tablespoon sour cream, chopped chives, parsley, green onion, grated Parmesan cheese, or crumbled crisp bacon.

Note Potato of uniform size will cook in the same length of time.

Baked in Coals

Scrub and rinse potatoes. Pierce potatoes with fork. Bury potatoes, unwrapped or wrapped in aluminum foil, in hot coals 45 to 60 minutes, or until easily pierced with fork. Skins will be black.

Basic Twice-Baked Potatoes

Makes 6 servings

    6 large Basic Baked Potatoes (see index), hot
    3 to 4 tablespoons butter or margarine
    ⅓ cup milk or light cream, heated
    1 teaspoon onion powder
    1 teaspoon salt
    ⅛ teaspoon white pepper
    2 egg whites
    ½ cup grated Swiss or cheddar cheese
      Paprika

Cut potatoes in half crosswise; carefully scoop out pulp, leaving a ¼-inch shell. Or, for larger shells, cut down through top of potato, removing only a small portion of top; carefully remove pulp. Place pulp in mixing bowl. Add butter, milk, onion powder, salt, and pepper. Beat with electric mixer until smooth; set aside. In small bowl, beat egg whites until stiff peaks form. Fold egg whites into potato mixture. Preheat oven to 400°F. Fill potato shells. Sprinkle with cheese and paprika. Bake for 10 minutes, or until cheese is melted.

Sour Cream Twice-Baked Potatoes

Combine 1 envelope (1½ ounces) sour cream mix, ¾ cup milk, salt, pepper, ½ teaspoon cumin, and 1 teaspoon butter in small bowl; blend well. Stir in potato pulp; blend well. Fill potato shells. Sprinkle with paprika. Bake as for Basic Twice-Baked Potatoes.

Cheese-Stuffed Twice-Baked Potatoes

Combine ½ cup milk and ¼ cup butter in small saucepan; heat until butter melts, stirring constantly. Stir into potato pulp. Add ½ cup sour cream, ½ cup cubed Swiss cheese, salt and pepper to taste. Fill shells. Bake at 350°F. 25 minutes. Top with ¼ cup shredded Swiss cheese, divided among potatoes. Return to oven until cheese melts.

Low-Calorie Twice-Baked Potatoes

Combine ⅔ cup hot water, 6 tablespoons nonfat dry milk powder, 1 tablespoon imitation butter, salt, and pepper in small bowl. Stir into potato pulp. Beat until fluffy and smooth. Fill shells. Sprinkle with paprika. Bake at 350°F. for 20 minutes. This recipe saves about 60 calories per potato.

Famished for Potatoes

It is no wonder, nutritionists tell us, that the 19th-century potato famine in Ireland caused such havoc. At that time, the diet in Ireland consisted mainly of potatoes and milk. That combination supplies most of the nutrients that the body needs, no matter how dull and monotonous a diet it would seem to be.

Twice-Baked Idaho Potatoes

Makes 4 servings

    4 Idaho® Potatoes
    ⅓ cup butter or margarine, divided
    2 cups sliced onions (2 medium)
    ⅓ cup plain yogurt
    1 tablespoon all-purpose flour
    1 egg
    1 teaspoon salt
      Paprika

Scrub potatoes, dry, and prick with a fork. Bake in 425°F. oven for 55 to 65 minutes, until soft. Meanwhile, melt ¼ cup butter in large skillet; add onions and cook until tender; set aside. When potatoes are cooked, cut slice from top of each; carefully scoop out pulp without breaking skin. Combine potato, yogurt, flour, egg and salt in large bowl; beat until smooth. Stir in reserved onion. Pile potato mixture into shells. Garnish each potato with remaining butter and sprinkle with paprika. Return to 350°F. oven and bake 25 to 30 minutes.

Idaho "Stanley Steamers"

Makes 4 servings

    4 Idaho® Potatoes
    8 slices bacon
    ½ cup chopped onion
    2 canned green chili peppers, drained, seeded,
        and chopped
    1 can (8 ounces) tomato sauce
    1 can (1 pound) tomatoes
    ½ teaspoon salt
    1 cup shredded cheddar cheese
    2 hard-cooked eggs

Scrub potatoes well. Place in large saucepan with 1-inch cold water. Bring water to boiling, reduce heat, and simmer covered 35 to 45 minutes, or until potatoes are tender. Drain. Meanwhile, in large skillet, cook bacon until golden brown; drain, crumble, and reserve. Pour off all but 2 tablespoons fat. Add onion; cook until tender. Add chili peppers, tomato sauce, tomatoes, salt, and half the crumbled bacon; cook 10 minutes. When potatoes are cool enough to handle, score skin lengthwise around center of potato; remove half of skin and discard. Arrange potatoes on heat-proof serving platter; top with prepared tomato sauce, and sprinkle with cheese. Place under broiler until cheese is just melted. Garnish with hard-cooked eggs and remaining bacon.

Lemon–Mustard–Stuffed Potatoes

Makes 4 servings

    4 Idaho® Potatoes
¼ cup butter or margarine
    1 cup chopped onion
    1 cup shredded carrot
    1 cup sliced mushrooms
¼ cup milk
    1 tablespoon lemon juice
    1 teaspoon prepared mustard
    1 teaspoon salt
¼ teaspoon pepper

Scrub potatoes, dry, and prick with a fork. Bake in a 425°F. oven 55 to 65 minutes, until soft. Reduce oven temperature to 350°F. When potatoes are done, cut a slice from top of each. Carefully scoop out potatoes without breaking skin. Set skins aside. Meanwhile, in medium saucepan melt butter; sauté onion, carrot, and mushrooms until soft. In large bowl, whip potatoes. Add milk, lemon juice, mustard, salt, and pepper; beat until smooth. Stir in sautéed vegetables. Spoon potato mixture into reserved potato skins. Bake in a 350°F. oven 20 to 30 minutes, until potatoes are heated through.

Mexicali-Stuffed Potatoes

Makes 4 servings

    4 Idaho® Potatoes
¾ cup tomato sauce
    2 tablespoons butter or margarine
½ teaspoon salt
½ teaspoon ground cumin
¾ cup whole-kernel corn, canned or frozen, thawed
    2 tablespoons chopped canned chilies
    2 tablespoons chopped parsley

Scrub potatoes, dry, and prick with a fork. Bake in a 425°F. oven 55 to 65 minutes, until soft. Reduce oven temperature to 350°F. When potatoes are done, cut slice from top of each. Carefully scoop out potato without breaking skin. Set skins aside. In medium mixing bowl, whip potatoes until smooth. Add tomato sauce, butter, salt, and cumin; beat until smooth. Stir in corn, chilies, and parsley. Spoon mixture into reserved potato skins. Bake in a 350°F. oven 20 to 30 minutes until potatoes are heated through.

Cheese-Stuffed Potatoes

Makes 6 servings

    6 baking potatoes
      Oil
    3 tablespoons butter or margarine
¼ cup chopped onion
    2 teaspoons Lea & Perrins Worcestershire Sauce
½ teaspoon salt
¾ cup shredded sharp cheddar cheese
      Paprika (optional)

Brush potatoes lightly with oil. Place on a baking sheet; bake in a preheated hot oven (400°F.) until potatoes are tender, about 1 hour. Cut potatoes in half lengthwise; carefully scoop out potato from skins. Mash potato with butter, onion, Lea & Perrins, and salt. Spoon mashed potato mixture into potato shells. Top with cheese. Return to hot oven and bake until cheese is melted, about 15 minutes. Sprinkle with paprika, if desired.

Specially Stuffed Spuds

Makes 12 servings

    6 large baking potatoes
    1 envelope Lipton® Onion-Mushroom or Onion Recipe Soup Mix
½ cup butter or margarine
¾ cup milk
      Garnishes: shredded cheddar or American cheese; crumbled, cooked bacon; chives; or buttered bread crumbs.

Bake potatoes until done. Split lengthwise and scoop out potatoes, reserving shells. Add Lipton Onion-Mushroom Recipe Soup Mix, butter, and at least ¾ cup milk; mash. Refill shells and top with one of the garnishes. Bake until heated through.

Reuben Baked Potatoes

Makes 4 servings

    4 large baking potatoes (about 2 pounds)
      Cooking oil
    1 can (7 ounces) SPAM®, diced
½ cup sauerkraut, rinsed and drained
½ cup shredded Swiss cheese

Wash potatoes well; rub with cooking oil. Bake in 425°F oven 45 minutes or until tender. Remove from oven; cut a cross in top and push ends together to open. Toss SPAM® with sauerkraut. Mound SPAM® mixture on top of potatoes; sprinkle with cheese. Return to oven for 5 to 7 minutes until SPAM® is hot and cheese melts.

Peel potatoes; grate coarsely, shred, or dice (4 cups). Melt butter in heavy 10-inch skillet. Sauté onion until transparent. Add potatoes, parsley, salt, and pepper. Do not pack potatoes down. Cook on moderate heat until golden brown and loosened from pan. Turn and brown other side. Serve hot.

Potatoes Anna

Makes 6 servings

- 4 **large potatoes, washed, peeled, and thinly sliced**
- 4 **tablespoons butter or margarine, melted, divided**
- 1 **teaspoon salt, divided**
- ½ **teaspoon freshly ground pepper, divided**

Preheat oven to 425°F. Generously grease a 10-inch pie plate. Beginning in center of pie plate, arrange potatoes in circles to edge of plate, overlapping slices. Pour 1 tablespoon butter over potatoes. Sprinkle on ¼ teaspoon salt and ⅛ teaspoon pepper. Repeat layers with remaining ingredients. Cover with aluminum foil. Bake 50 minutes, or until potatoes are tender and golden brown. Drain butter. Carefully turn potatoes upside down onto serving plate. Serve immediately.

Potatoes Basil

Makes 4 servings

- ½ **small onion, finely chopped**
- 1 **small clove garlic, crushed**
- 2 **tablespoons Italian dressing**
- 3 **medium potatoes, washed, peeled, and cut into 1-inch cubes**
- ½ **green pepper, seeded and chopped**
- 1 **cup cherry tomatoes, halved**
- ½ **teaspoon salt**
- 1 **tablespoon chopped fresh basil or ¾ teaspoon dried basil**

Combine onion, garlic, and salad dressing in small skillet. Cook on moderate heat 5 minutes, or until onion is transparent. Add potatoes and ½ cup water. Cover and cook on low heat 10 minutes. Cover and cook on low heat 15 minutes, or until potatoes and green pepper are tender. Stir in tomatoes, salt, and basil. Cover and cook 5 minutes, or until tomatoes are heated through. Serve hot.

Basque Potato Soup (page 56); Idaho Stanley Steamers (page 112); Twice-Baked Idaho Potatoes (page 112). Idaho Potato Commission

Potatoes Anna; Potatoes Basil. Wisconsin Potato Growers Auxiliary

Hash Browns

Makes 6 servings

- 6 **medium Basic Baked Potatoes (see index), baked at least the day before and refrigerated**
- ⅓ **cup butter, margarine, bacon fat, or vegetable shortening**
- 1 **medium onion, thinly sliced**
- 1 **tablespoon parsley flakes**
- 1 **teaspoon salt**
- ¼ **teaspoon pepper**

Au Gratin Pumpkin Bake

Makes 6 to 8 servings

1½ cups milk
1 cup Libby's Solid Pack Pumpkin
4 ounces cream cheese, softened
¼ cup grated Parmesan cheese
¾ teaspoon salt
¼ teaspoon pepper
4 Idaho potatoes, peeled and thinly sliced
6 slices bacon, crisply cooked and crumbled
½ cup green onion slices

Preheat oven to 425°F. In blender container, combine milk, pumpkin, cream cheese, Parmesan cheese, salt, and pepper. Blend at medium speed until smooth. Blend at high speed for 2 minutes, or until light and fluffy. In a large bowl, combine potato slices, bacon, and green onion. Pour pumpkin mixture over potatoes; toss lightly until well-coated. Pour into lightly buttered 11¾x7½-inch baking dish. Cover with foil; bake 55 minutes. Remove foil; continue baking 5 minutes. Let stand 5 minutes before serving.

Cranberry Acorn Squash

Makes 4 servings

2 small acorn squash, halved and seeded
2 tablespoons dark brown sugar
¼ teaspoon ground cinnamon
1 can (16 ounces) whole cranberry sauce

Preheat oven to 350°F. Place large-size (14x20 inches) Reynolds Oven Cooking Bag in 12x8x2-inch baking dish. Sprinkle squash with brown sugar and cinnamon. Fill squash with cranberry sauce; place in bag. Close bag with nylon tie; make 6 ½-inch slits in top. Cook 45 to 55 minutes, or until squash is tender.

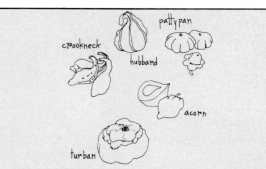

Succulent Squash Selection

There are two main squash types, summer and winter, and a number of varieties of each. Following are summer squashes:

Caserta: Striped light and dark green, the caserta is shaped like the cocozelle, but thicker. Best when 6 or 7 inches long and 1 to 1½ inches thick.

Chayote: Shaped like a pear and about the size of an acorn squash, the chayote is pale green and, unlike other squash, has only one central seed, which is edible. Its flavor is very delicate. Do not peel.

Cocozelle: A smooth or slightly ribbed cylindrical squash striped dark green and yellow, with a flavor rather like zucchini. Best when 6 to 8 inches long, 2 inches in diameter.

Cymling (also called scallop or pattypan): Skin may be smooth or somewhat bumpy; pale green when young, it turns white as the squash matures. The vegetable is shaped like a dish and has a scalloped edge. Best when 3 to 4 inches across.

Yellow crookneck and straightneck: Yellow, somewhat bumpy skin that grows deeper in color as the vegetable matures. At their best when about half mature, while skin is still soft enough so that the squash does not need to be peeled. The crookneck can grow to 10 inches in length, the straightneck to 20, but they are much preferable before they reach maturity.

Zucchini: Cylindrical, but often somewhat larger at the base; the skin has wide dark green stripes alternating with narrow pale green ones. Can grow to 12 inches in length, but best when less mature—4 to 5 inches long.

All winter squashes are green or orange in color, with a hard, tough skin. These are the common varieties:

Acorn (also known as table queen and Des Moines): Deeply ribbed dark green skin that may turn orange in storage. Orange flesh. Grows 5 to 8 inches in length, 4 to 5 inches thick.

Buttercup: Rises to a turban-shaped mound at the blossom end. Skin is dark green with marks and some stripes of pale gray. Flesh is dry but sweet, orange in color. Grows 4 to 5 inches long, 6 to 8 inches thick, with a 2- to 3-inch turban.

Butternut: Cylindrical, tapering to a bulbous end. Skin is smooth, generally buff colored. Flesh is orange, sweet, moist. Grows to 12 inches in length, up to 5 inches thick at the bulb.

Hubbard: Globe shaped with a tapered neck, grows up to 12 inches in length. The warty skin is varied—a dusty blue-gray, a deep green, an orange that leans toward red. The flesh is sweet, usually moist, and yellow-orange.

Turban: Shaped like a drum, with a turban-shaped end like the buttercup's. Bumpy skin of the squash proper is orange with stripes at the blossom end, of the turban blue-green. Grows to 10 inches in length, 15 in diameter.

Praline Acorn Squash

Makes 4 servings

 2 medium acorn squash, halved lengthwise, seeds removed
 ½ cup water
 ¼ cup Land O Lakes Sweet Cream Butter, softened
 ⅓ cup chopped pecans
 ¼ cup firmly packed brown sugar
 ¼ teaspoon mace
 2 teaspoons vanilla extract

Heat oven to 400°F. In greased 12x8-inch baking dish, place squash cut side up. Pour water in dish; set aside. In small bowl stir together remaining ingredients. Divide mixture evenly among squash halves.

Candied Sweet Potatoes

Makes 6 servings

 ¼ cup butter or margarine
 1 cup firmly packed brown sugar
 ¼ cup orange juice
 ½ teaspoon salt
 1 teaspoon grated orange rind or ground cinnamon
 6 cooked medium sweet potatoes, peeled and cut in half lengthwise
   Chopped nuts (optional)

Preheat Sunbeam Multi-Cooker Frypan to 320°F. Combine butter, brown sugar, juice, salt and rind in Frypan. Boil, stirring, about 2 minutes. Add sweet potatoes to syrup and simmer 10 minutes at about 220°F., frequently spooning syrup over potatoes and turning them. Serve hot; garnish with chopped nuts, if desired.

Baked Orange-Sweet Potatoes

Makes 6 servings

 2 cans (18 ounces each) sweet potatoes, drained
 ¼ cup butter or margarine
 1 small unpeeled orange, cut up
 ⅓ cup firmly packed brown sugar
 ¼ teaspoon salt
   Dash ground nutmeg
   Dash ground ginger

Heat oven to 350°F. Slice sweet potatoes into 9x9x2-inch baking dish. Put remaining ingredients into blender container in order listed. Cover; blend at medium speed until orange is finely chopped. If necessary, stop blender during processing and push ingredients toward blades with rubber spatula. Spoon mixture over sweet potatoes. Bake 30 minutes.

Hawaiian Sweet Potatoes

Makes about 4 servings

 1 can (17 ounces) sweet potatoes, drained
 ¼ cup Wish-Bone® Deluxe French Dressing
 1 can (8 ounces) crushed pineapple, drained
 2 tablespoons shredded coconut
 2 tablespoons brown sugar

Preheat oven to 400°F. In medium bowl, mash sweet potatoes; blend in Wish-Bone Deluxe French Dressing and pineapple. Turn into 1-quart casserole and sprinkle with coconut and brown sugar. Bake 25 to 30 minutes.

Creamed Spinach

Makes 4 servings

 1 package (10 ounces) fresh spinach
 1 thin slice onion
 1 cup milk
 3 tablespoons softened butter or margarine
 3 tablespoons all-purpose flour
 ½ teaspoon salt
 ⅛ teaspoon pepper
 ⅛ teaspoon ground nutmeg

Wash spinach well; shake off excess water; pat dry. Remove coarse stems and discard; tear large leaves into pieces. Put all ingredients except spinach into blender container in order listed. Cover; blend at medium speed until onion is very finely chopped. While blender is running, tip center cap and gradually add spinach, blending until chopped. Turn into saucepan. Cook over low heat, stirring frequently, 5 to 7 minutes.

Celery-Creamed Spinach

Makes 4 to 6 servings

 2 pounds fresh spinach or 2 packages (10 ounces each) frozen chopped spinach
 1 can (10½ ounces) Campbell's Condensed Cream of Celery Soup
 ⅓ cup light cream
   Dash ground nutmeg

Wash fresh spinach in several changes of water to remove all sand. Place in a large kettle with a small amount of water and cook covered until spinach is wilted and just tender. Drain, pressing out all liquid, then chop. (If using frozen spinach, cook as directed on package, and press out all liquid.) Combine spinach, soup, cream, and nutmeg in a saucepan. Heat until mixture bubbles.

Scalloped Tomatoes. Caloric Corporation

Tomatoes Provençal

Makes 4 servings

    4 **medium tomatoes**
    ½ **teaspoon salt**
    ¼ **teaspoon pepper**
    2 **slices dry bread**
    2 **tablespoons softened butter or margarine**
    ½ **clove garlic**
    ¼ **cup parsley sprigs**
    1 **teaspoon Dijon-style mustard**

Heat oven to 375°F. Cut tomatoes in half horizontally. Arrange halves, cut side up, in greased shallow baking pan. Sprinkle with salt and pepper. Spread each slice of bread with 1 tablespoon butter. Break bread slices into blender container. Cover; blend at medium speed until crumbed. Add garlic, parsley, and mustard. Cover; blend at medium speed until parsley is chopped and mixture is combined. Sprinkle mixture over tomato halves. Bake 20 minutes.

Scalloped Tomatoes

Makes 4 to 6 servings

    1 **pound very ripe tomatoes, peeled and sliced**
    1 **onion, thinly sliced**
    1 **cup fresh bread crumbs**
    ¼ **cup grated Parmesan cheese**
    ½ **teaspoon basil**
    ½ **teaspoon salt**
    ⅛ **teaspoon freshly ground pepper**
    2 **tablespoons butter or margarine**
       Chopped scallions

Layer half of the tomatoes in lightly greased 1½-quart casserole. Top with half of the onions. Combine bread crumbs, Parmesan cheese, basil, salt, and pepper. Sprinkle half the crumb mixture over the onions. Repeat tomato and onion layers. Sprinkle with remaining crumb mixture and dot with butter. Preheat oven to 400°F. Cover casserole and bake 40 minutes, or until hot and bubbly. Remove cover and bake 5 to 10 minutes, until topping is lightly browned. Sprinkle with scallions.

Scalloped Zucchini (page 120); Stuffed Eggplant (page 36).
Campbell Soup Company

Basil Tomatoes

Makes 8 servings

  3 to 4 beefsteak tomatoes
  ¼ cup olive oil
  3 tablespoons wine vinegar
    Sugar
  2 teaspoons crumbled basil
    Salt and freshly ground black pepper to taste

Cut tomatoes into ¼-inch slices. Lay slices, slightly overlapping, in an attractive pattern on a serving platter. Mix oil, vinegar, and pinch of sugar. Sprinkle over tomatoes. Sprinkle with basil, then with salt, and finish with a few grindings of pepper. Refrigerate at least 1 hour.

Scalloped Zucchini

Makes 6 servings

  4 large zucchini, cut into round slices ½ inch
    wide
  4 hard-cooked eggs, chopped
  1 can (10¾ ounces) Campbell's Condensed
    Cheddar Cheese Soup
  ⅓ cup heavy cream
  ½ cup grated sharp cheddar cheese
  ¼ cup flavored dry bread crumbs

Layer zucchini and eggs alternately in a greased 8-inch square pan. The top layer should be eggs. Mix soup and cream; spoon evenly over casserole. Sprinkle top with cheese and bread crumbs. Bake in a preheated 350°F. oven for 40 to 45 minutes, or until zucchini is easily pierced with a fork and the top of the casserole is lightly browned.

Tomatoes: Every Day and Every Way

Fruits that we treat as vegetables, fresh tomatoes are available everywhere throughout the year, shipped in from warmer climates to cold-weather areas in winter. The fruit can be picked when mature but still green, and will ripen in transit or while warehoused. Vine-ripened tomatoes, however, have better flavor. Some tomatoes are grown hydroponically, in large tanks that are periodically flooded with water to which nutrients have been added. This growing method is more costly, but the crop is considerably greater than that harvested from tomato plants conventionally grown in soil.

There are an almost infinite number of ways to prepare and serve tomatoes.

To remove the skins from fresh tomatoes, impale on the tines of a fork at the stem end, immerse in boiling water for ½ minute, then dip in cold water. With the point of a sharp knife, peel the tomato—the skin will slip off easily and neatly. Another method: rotate the impaled tomato over an open flame until the skin wrinkles; it will then peel readily. Sometimes it's necessary to peel tomatoes, but don't do it unless it's required— that skin supplies "roughage," the fiber needed in a balanced diet.

Stuffed tomatoes, raw or cooked, seem to be well liked by almost everyone. Stuff the raw ones with a salad mixture of vegetables, chicken, shrimp, tuna, or any other you'd like to use. Tomatoes are an accommodatingly compatible flavor with almost any other food. If you want to serve more salad than the slightly hollowed-out tomato will hold, cut the tomato into 6 to 8 petals, slicing through the skin to within ½ inch of the bottom; spread the petals, and you'll have a larger area to stuff. In either case, first invert the tomatoes on absorbent paper to drain. Cooked stuffed tomatoes may be filled with another vegetable or a mixture, with creamed foods, or with the removed pulp combined with chopped mushrooms and butter-sautéed bread crumbs.

Sliced beefsteak tomatoes (cut with a knife that has a serrated or scalloped blade) are delicious sprinkled with oil and vinegar; then with a mixture of ½ salt, ¼ sugar, and ¼ coarsely ground black pepper; then with coarsely chopped fresh basil. Or slice and serve as individual salads on beds of watercress, with mayonnaise on the side; let each diner season his own portion.

Broiled tomatoes are excellent with any kind of broiled meat or poultry. Halve the tomatoes, then make a number of shallow slits on each cut surface. Season with salt and pepper, top liberally with a mixture of melted butter, bread or cracker crumbs, and grated cheddar or Parmesan. Broil until lightly browned.

Fried tomatoes, green ones or ripe, are a farm-style favorite. Cut in ½-inch slices. Dip green tomatoes into seasoned flour and cook slowly in hot fat. Dip ripe ones into beaten egg, then into dry bread or cracker crumbs, cook quickly in hot fat. Bacon drippings are a very good fat in which to fry tomatoes. Season the slices after cooking.

Basil, thyme, rosemary, summer savory, and marjoram all complement the flavor of both raw and cooked tomatoes. Bacon, mushrooms, shrimp, chicken, eggplant, and beans are all naturals with the fruit. And in any cooked tomato dish, remember always to add a very small amount of sugar, which cuts the acid taste and mellows the flavor.

Stir-Fried Zucchini

Makes 4 to 6 servings

    4 baby zucchini, sliced ½ inch thick
    ½ cup walnut pieces
    1 red bell pepper, cut into 3x½-inch strips
    1 green bell pepper, cut into 3x½-inch strips
      Salt and coarsely ground black pepper
    2 tablespoons vegetable oil
    ½ cup chicken broth (canned)
    1 tablespoon cornstarch
    ½ cup Seven Seas Viva® Red Wine Vinegar & Oil
      dressing
      Grated Parmesan cheese (optional)

In wok or large nonstick skillet, stir-fry vegetables and walnuts in oil; season with salt and pepper. In small cup, combine dressing, broth, and cornstarch; stir well and add to skillet. Heat and stir until sauce thickens. Serve with grated Parmesan cheese, if desired.

Roman Zucchini

Makes 6 servings

    4 medium tomatoes, peeled, cored, and cut up
    1 medium onion, cut up
    ½ green pepper, seeded and cut up
    1 stalk celery, cut up
    1 clove garlic, halved
    ½ teaspoon salt
    6 small zucchini (about 1½ pounds), sliced
    2 tablespoons butter or margarine

Put tomatoes into blender container. Cover; blend at low speed until pureéd. Add onion, green pepper, celery, garlic, and salt. Cover; blend at medium speed until vegetables are chopped. Empty into large skillet. Add zucchini and butter. Simmer covered 10 to 15 minutes, stirring occasionally, until zucchini is tender.

Skillet Zucchini

Makes 4 to 6 servings

    ¼ cup butter or margarine
    6 small zucchini, cut into ¼-inch slices
    1 onion, thinly sliced
    1 teaspoon salt
      Dash pepper
    2 tomatoes, cut into chunks
    ¼ cup shredded cheddar cheese
    1 tablespoon soy sauce

Heat Sunbeam Multi-Cooker Frypan to 300°F. Melt butter; add zucchini, onion, seasonings, tomatoes, and ¼ cup water. Cook covered 10 minutes. Sprinkle with cheddar and soy sauce; cook covered 2 minutes.

Italian Fried Zucchini

Makes 6 to 8 servings

    1¾ cups all-purpose flour
    ¾ cup milk
    2 eggs
    ½ teaspoon salt
    ⅛ teaspoon ground nutmeg
      Pepper to taste
      Pinch Cayenne pepper
    4 small zucchini, sliced into thin strips
    3 cups seasoned bread crumbs
    ½ cup grated Parmesan cheese
      Vegetable oil
    1 jar (15½ ounces) Ragú Chunky Gardenstyle
      Spaghetti Sauce, heated

In a blender, combine first 7 ingredients; blend 1 minute, or until batter is smooth. In a large bowl, pour batter over zucchini. Toss to evenly coat; set aside. In a large bowl, combine bread crumbs and cheese. Dip zucchini into bread crumb mixture. In a large skillet, fry zucchini in hot oil in small batches; drain on paper towels. Serve immediately with heated spaghetti sauce.

Zucchini Crunch

Makes 4 servings

    1 pound zucchini, sliced
    1 tablespoon Lea & Perrins Worcestershire Sauce
    4 tablespoons butter or margarine
      Pignola nuts, toasted

In a saucepan, combine all ingredients except nuts. Cook covered for 12 minutes. Remove to platter; sprinkle with toasted pignola nuts.

Zucchini with Herbs

Makes 4 to 6 servings

    6 small zucchini, sliced into 1-inch pieces
    2 medium onion, thinly sliced
    2 cloves garlic, minced
    ¼ cup olive oil
    1 jar (15½ ounces) Ragú Chunky Gardenstyle
      Spaghetti Sauce
    1 teaspoon minced fresh parsley
    ½ teaspoon oregano
    ½ teaspoon basil
    ¼ teaspoon thyme
      Salt to taste
      Pepper to taste
      Grated Parmesan cheese

In a large skillet, lightly sauté zucchini, onions, and garlic in oil. Add spaghetti sauce, parsley, oregano, basil, thyme, salt, and pepper. Simmer covered 15 minutes, or until zucchini is tender, stirring occasionally. Sprinkle with cheese.

Calico Corn Relish
Put up by: _____
Date: _____

Put up by:

To Complement Your Taste

Pickles and relishes—all those extra-good, extra-flavorful foods whose mission is to make the other menu items taste and look even better.

Horseradish-Beet Relish

Makes 1½ cups
   1 tablespoon vinegar
   1 tablespoon sugar
   1 can (16 ounces) diced beets, drained
   ⅛ teaspoon pepper
   1 teaspoon salt
   ¼ cup prepared horseradish, drained

Put all ingredients into blender container in order listed. Cover; blend at medium speed just until beets are finely chopped. Refrigerate 2 to 3 days.
Serving suggestion: Serve with roast beef, pork, lamb, tongue, or corned beef.

Patio Pepper Relish

Makes about 7 cups
   4 cups shredded cabbage
   1 cup finely chopped green pepper
   1 cup finely chopped red pepper
   1 cup finely chopped celery
   ¼ cup finely chopped green onions
   ⅔ cup Wish-Bone® Italian Dressing

In large bowl, combine cabbage, peppers, celery, and green onions; toss with Wish-Bone Italian Dressing. Cover and marinate in refrigerator, stirring occasionally, 4 hours or overnight. Store in refrigerator up to 1 week.

Patio Pepper Relish; Italian Tomato Salad Topping; Calico Corn Relish. Photo courtesy of Thomas J. Lipton, Inc.

Italian Tomato Salad Topping

Toss this colorful mixture with greens for instant salad.

Makes about 4 cups
   2 cups coarsely chopped tomato
   1 cup chopped red onion
   1 cup diagonally sliced celery
   ½ cup Wish-Bone® Italian Dressing
   2 tablespoons dry red wine
   1 tablespoon chopped fresh basil or 1 teaspoon dry basil

In large bowl, combine tomato, onion, and celery; add Wish-Bone Italian Dressing blended with wine and basil. Spoon into 1-quart jar; secure lid tightly and chill, inverting jar occasionally, 4 hours or overnight. Store in refrigerator up to 1 week.

Calico Corn Relish

Makes about 4 cups
   ½ cup Wish-Bone® Russian Dressing
   2½ cups cooked corn
   1 cup thinly sliced celery
   ½ cup finely chopped onion
   ¼ cup finely chopped pimiento

In large bowl, combine all ingredients. Cover and marinate in refrigerator, stirring occasionally, 4 hours or overnight.

Quick Garden Relish

Makes about 5 cups

½ medium head green cabbage, coarsely cut up
2 carrots, pared and cut up
1 green pepper, seeded and cut up
1 medium onion, cut up
¾ cup cider vinegar
¾ cup sugar
2 teaspoons salt
½ teaspoon mustard seed
½ teaspoon celery seed

Fill blender container to 5-cup mark with cut-up vegetables. Add cold water to cover vegetables. Cover; blend at medium speed just until vegetables are chopped. Drain thoroughly in colander; return any large pieces to blender container. Empty vegetables from colander into bowl. Repeat procedure until all vegetables are chopped. Put remaining ingredients into blender container in order listed. Cover; blend at low speed until mixed. Pour over chopped vegetables; mix well. Refrigerate at least 2 hours before serving.

Raw Mushroom Relish

Makes 1 cup

10 medium-size mushrooms, quartered
2 scallions, sliced (including some green)
¼ cup Sun-Maid® Seedless Golden Raisins
½ teaspoon salt
½ teaspoon oregano
2 tablespoons white wine vinegar
⅛ teaspoon hot pepper sauce

Place all the ingredients in a food processor (use chopping blade) or blender container and turn on and off quickly to finely chop the ingredients without making a purée. Chill before serving.

Relish for Franks 'n' Burgers

Makes about 2½ cups

¾ cup Wish-Bone® Russian Dressing
1 tablespoon cornstarch
2 to 3 teaspoons dry mustard
1½ cups finely chopped green pepper
1 cup finely chopped cucumber, drained
1 cup finely chopped celery
½ cup finely chopped onion
2 tablespoons chopped pimiento

In small bowl, blend Wish-Bone Russian Dressing, cornstarch, and mustard.

In large saucepan, combine green pepper, cucumber, celery, onion, pimiento, and dressing mixture. Bring to a boil, then simmer 5 minutes, stirring frequently, until mixture is slightly thickened. Spoon into covered container; secure lid tightly and chill. Store in refrigerator up to 1 week.

Sweet Honey Gherkins

Makes about 6 pints

48 small cucumbers, 1½ inches long
4 quarts boiling water
3¾ cups vinegar
3 cups Sue Bee Honey
3 tablespoons salt
4½ teaspoons celery seed
4½ teaspoons turmeric
¾ teaspoon mustard seed

Wash cucumbers and put them in a stone jar or enamel kettle. Pour over boiling water to cover and let stand 4 to 5 hours. Drain cucumbers and pack in sterilized pint jars. Combine vinegar, Sue Bee Honey, and remaining ingredients and boil 5 minutes. Pour boiling hot syrup over cucumbers, leaving ½ inch headspace. Remove air bubbles and wipe rims. Adjust lids firmly and process 5 minutes in boiling water bath.

Carrot Pickles

Makes 3 pints

   3 **pounds carrots**
   1 **cup Sue Bee Honey**
   2 **cups white vinegar**
   1 **teaspoon salt**
   ½ **tablespoon whole cloves**
   ½ **tablespoon allspice**
   ½ **tablespoon mace**
   1 **cinnamon stick, broken in pieces**

Wash and scrape carrots and cut in strips of desired size. Cook carrots about 3 minutes, or until tender. Combine Sue Bee Honey, vinegar, and salt and add to carrots. Tie spices in cheesecloth bag. Add to carrot mixture. Boil 5 to 8 minutes. Remove spice bag. Pack carrots into hot, sterilized pint jars, leaving ¼ inch headspace. Release air bubbles and wipe rims. Adjust lids firmly and process 30 minutes in boiling water bath.

Pint o' Pickles

Makes 1 pint

   ½ **cup cider vinegar**
   ¼ **cup sugar**
   ½ **teaspoon mustard seed**
   ½ **teaspoon salt**
   ⅛ **teaspoon celery seed**
      Dash turmeric
   2½ **cups sliced cucumbers**
   1 **small onion, thinly sliced**

Combine vinegar, water, sugar, mustard seed, salt, celery seed, and turmeric in small saucepan. Heat to boiling, stirring constantly. Boil 5 minutes. Add cucumbers and onion. Heat to simmering. Simmer 10 minutes, or until cucumber slices are tender-crisp. Let stand covered 10 minutes. Spoon into container, cover, and chill before serving.

This recipe was provided by Saran Wrap™ brand plastic film.

Pickle Pointers

Pickling can be done at home with relative ease at times when vegetables are at their peak season (highest quality, lowest price), and laid away for the bleaker months. They are water-bath processed, which goes from cooking kettle to container without processing. Some pickles are cured in brine (fermented) before being processed.

Follow up-to-date recipes in making pickles for most satisfactory results. Read the recipe carefully before you shop for ingredients, to make certain that you will have everything you need on hand. Alum and lime are not used in modern pickling—if top-quality ingredients are used and a reliable recipe followed, there is no need for them.

Salt: If it is available, use pure granulated salt. Table salt may be used, but ingredients added to table salt to prevent caking may make pickle brine cloudy. Under no circumstances use iodized salt—it turns pickles dark.

Vinegar: Use high-grade cider or distilled white vinegar. The flavor of cider vinegar is preferable, but white may be called for in recipes for pale-colored pickles, such as cauliflower or pears. Never dilute the vinegar unless the recipe directs you to do so; if you prefer a less sour pickle, add sugar rather than decreasing vinegar.

Water: Soft water must be used for pickle brine. If your water is hard, boil it for 15 minutes; let it stand 24 hours, then skim it carefully and ladle out the water rather than pouring it, so that the sediment on the bottom is not disturbed. Before using, add 1 tablespoon vinegar to each gallon of boiled water.

Cucumbers: Make certain the ones you buy (which should be pickling, not salad varieties) have not been waxed. The brine cannot penetrate the wax coating, and the pickles will be spoiled.

Heat pickle liquids in kettles of unchipped enamelware, stainless steel, aluminum, or glass. Copper, brass, galvanized, or iron vessels may react with the acids and cause undesirable changes in the pickles. For fermenting or brining, use crocks or stone or glass jars, or large stoneware or glass bowls.

For successful pickle making, you will need a kitchen scale, as many ingredients are measured by weight rather than by volume. You will need, as well, a large water-bath kettle, canning jars and their closures, large wooden or stainless steel spoons for stirring, measuring cups, sharp knives, a large-mouth funnel, a large ladle with pouring lip, tongs or jar lifter, a footed colander, a food grinder, and a cutting board.

But most of all you need the desire to make pickles and good, modern recipes that you will follow to the last dotting of *i* and crossing of *t*. Armed with those, you can produce such homemade good things as sauerkraut, dilled beans, icicle pickles, pickled zucchini, artichoke relish, chow-chow, picalilli, corn relish, chili sauce, pickled pears, spiced peaches, tomato catsup, pickled figs, sweet crab apple pickles, peach chutney, watermelon rind pickles, and dozens more.

Sweet Pepper Relish (page 126). Hamilton Beach Scovill Inc.

Sweet Pepper Relish

Makes 4½ pints

  12 medium green peppers, seeded and cut up
  12 medium sweet red peppers, seeded and cut up
   4 medium onions, cut up
      Boiling water
   2 cups cider vinegar
1¾ cups sugar
   1 tablespoon salt
   1 teaspoon mustard seed

Fill blender container to 5-cup mark with cut-up vegetables. Add cold water to cover vegetables. Cover; blend at medium speed just until vegetables are chopped. Drain thoroughly in colander; return any large pieces to blender container. Empty vegetables from colander into large saucepan. Repeat procedure until all vegetables are chopped. Pour boiling water over vegetables in saucepan to cover; let stand 15 minutes. Drain in colander 4 to 5 hours. Return vegetables to saucepan. Add vinegar, sugar, salt, and mustard seed. Heat to boiling; reduce heat; simmer uncovered 20 minutes. Ladle into hot sterilized pint jars. Seal at once.

Salsa

Makes about 4 cups

   1 pound ripe tomatoes, chopped (2½ cups)
  ½ cup coarsely chopped onion
  ½ cup coarsely chopped celery
  ½ cup coarsely chopped green pepper
   4 tablespoons Mazola Corn Oil
   1 can (4 ounces) chopped hot green chilies, drained (¼ cup)
   2 tablespoons red wine vinegar
   2 tablespoons chopped parsley
   1 clove garlic, minced or pressed
  ½ teaspoon salt
  ⅛ teaspoon crushed dried red pepper

In medium bowl, stir together tomatoes, onion, celery, green pepper, corn oil, chilies, vinegar, parsley, garlic, salt, and pepper until well mixed. Cover; refrigerate several hours, or overnight. Serve as a relish.

Index